Practicing Faith and Faithfulness

Practicing Faith and Faithfulness

Introduction to Spiritual Formation

under the supervision of
Mark A. Maddix

Theological Essentials

Library of Congress Cataloging-in-Publication Data

Mark A. Maddix (creator).
Practicing Faith and Faithfulness: An Introduction to Spiritual Formation / Mark A. Maddix
136 + *xiv* pp. cm. 12.7 x 20.32
ISBN 979-8-89731-298-6 (Print)
ISBN 979-8-89731-290-0 (Ebook)
ISBN 979-8-89731-282-5 (Kindle)
ISBN 979-8-89731-274-0 (Abridged Audio Discussion)

1. Spiritual formation.
2. Christian life.
3. Faith—Practice.

BV4501.3 .M33 2026

This book is available in other languages at www.DTLPress.com

Cover Image: "A Journey of Faith and Faithfulness"
Cover Credit: DTL staff, using Artificial Intelligence

Contents

Section II
Relationship with Others

Section III
Relationship with Self

Series Preface

Artificial Intelligence (AI) is changing everything, including theological scholarship and education. This series, *Theological Essentials,* is designed to bring the creative potential of AI to the field of theological education. In the traditional model, a scholar with both mastery of the scholarly discourse and a record of successful classroom teaching would spend several months—or even several years—writing, revising and rewriting an introductory text which would then be transferred to a publisher who also invested months or years in production processes. Even though the end product was typically quite predictable, this slow and expensive process caused the prices of textbooks to balloon. As a result, students in developed nations paid more than they should have for the books and students in developing nations typically had no access to these (cost-prohibitive) textbooks until they appeared as discards and donations decades later. In previous generations, the need for quality assurance—in the form of content generation, expert review, copy-editing and printing time—may have made this slow, expensive and exclusionary approach inevitable. However, AI is changing everything.

This series is very different; it is created by AI. The cover of each volume identifies the work as "created under the supervision of" an expert in the field. However, that person is not an author in the traditional sense. The creator of each volume has been trained by the DTL staff in the use of AI and *the creator has used AI to create, edit, revise and recreate the text that you see.* With that creation process clearly identified, let me explain the goals of this series.

Our Goals:

Credibility: Although AI has made—and continues to make—huge strides over the last few years, no unsupervised AI can create a truly reliable or fully credible college or seminary level text. The limitations of AI generated content sometimes originates from the limitations of the content itself (the training set may be inadequate), but more often, user dissatisfaction with AI-generated content arises from human errors associated with poor prompt engineering. The DTL Press has sought to overcome both of these problems by hiring established scholars with widely recognized expertise to create books within their areas of expertise and by training those scholars and experts in AI prompt engineering. To be clear, the scholar whose name appears on the cover of this work has created this volume—generating, reading, regenerating, rereading and revising the work. Even though the work was generated (in varying degrees) by AI, the names of our scholarly creators appear on the cover as a guarantee that the content is equally credible with any introductory work which that scholar/creator would pen using the traditional model.

Stability: AI is generative, meaning that the response to each prompt is uniquely generated for that specific request. No two AI-generated responses are precisely the same. The inevitable variability of AI responses presents a significant pedagogical challenge for professors and students who wish to begin their discussions and analysis on the basis of a shared set of ideas. Educational institutions need stable texts in order to prevent pedagogical chaos. These books provide that stable text from which to teach, discuss and engage ideas.

Affordability: The DTL Press is committed to the idea that affordability should not be a barrier to knowledge. *All persons are equally deserving of the right to know and to understand.* Therefore, ebook versions of all DTL Press books are available from the DTL libraries without charge, and available as print books for a nominal fee. Our scholar/creators are to be thanked for their willingness to forego traditional royalty arrangements. (Our creators are compensated for their generative work, but they do not receive royalties in the traditional sense.)

Accessibility: The DTL Press would like to make high quality, low cost introductory textbooks available to everyone, everywhere in the world. The books in this series are immediately made available in multiple languages. The DTL Press will create translations in other languages upon request. Translations are, of course, generated by AI.

Our Acknowledged Limitations:

Some readers are undoubtedly thinking, "but AI can only produce derivative scholarship;

AI can't create original, innovative scholarship." That criticism is, of course, largely accurate. AI is largely limited to aggregating, organizing and repackaging pre-existing ideas (although sometimes in ways that can be used to accelerate and refine the production of original scholarship). Still while acknowledging this inherent limitation of AI, the DTL Press would offer two comments: (1) Introductory texts are seldom meant to be truly ground breaking in their originality and (2) the DTL Press has other series dedicated to publishing original scholarship with traditional authorship.

Our Invitation:

The DTL Press would like to fundamentally reshape academic publishing in the theological world to make scholarship more accessible and more affordable in two ways. First, we would like to generate introductory texts in all areas of theological discourse, so that no one is ever forced to "buy a textbook" in any language. It is our vision for professors anywhere to be able to use one book, two books or an entire set of books in this series as the *introductory* textbooks for their classes. Second, we would also like to publish traditionally authored scholarly monographs for Open Access (free) distribution for an advanced scholarly readership.

Finally, the DTL Press is non-confessional and will publish works in any area of religious studies. Traditionally authored books are peer-reviewed; AI-generated introductory book creation is open to anyone with the required expertise to supervise content generation in that area of discourse. If you share the DTL Press's commitment to credibility, affordability and accessibility, contact us about changing the world of theological publishing by contributing to this series or a more traditionally authored series.

With high expectations,
Thomas E. Phillips
DTL Press Executive Director
www.thedtl.org
www.DTLpress.com

Introduction

The Journey of Being Formed

I remember the first time I felt the stir deep in my soul: a quiet longing, a sense that there was more to this faith than Sunday rituals and religious language. I would read a passage of Scripture and for a moment, the words pulsed with life: You are loved. Or I would drop to my knees in prayer and feel God's presence, like breath in my lungs, calling me out of the surface and into the depths.

That stirring, that longing, is the beginning of a journey. A journey not of achievement, but of formation. Not merely of knowledge, but of becoming.

What I gradually discovered, sometimes painfully, often joyfully, is that my faith was never meant to remain surface-level. The Christian life is not simply about believing the right things or doing the right things; it's about becoming someone who reflects the very heart of Christ.

What Is Christian Spiritual Formation?

Christian spiritual formation is the ongoing, grace-filled process of being conformed to the image of Jesus Christ for the glory of God and the good of the world. It is grounded in Scripture, empowered by the Holy Spirit, and centered on the person of Jesus. As Paul writes in Romans 8:29, we are "predestined to be conformed to the image of his Son."

This formation isn't just external behavior modification. It's internal transformation. It's the shaping of the heart, mind, body, and will into alignment with God's character so that we live not merely for Christ, but from His life within us (Galatians 2:20).

Reflection #1: *Where are you now?*

Take a moment to describe your current spiritual life. Are you feeling close to God, distant, dry, curious, or restless? Be honest. This isn't about where you should be, but where you truly are.

Christian spiritual formation happens through intentional practices of prayer, silence, Scripture, worship, and service, but these are not ends in themselves. They are means by which we create space for God to do what only He can: renew our minds (Romans 12:2), transform our hearts (Ezekiel 36:26), and restore our identity in Christ (Colossians 3:10).

Why It Matters For You, For Me, For the World

We are all being formed, all the time by culture, by media, by our past, and by our habits. The question isn't if we're being formed. The question is into what?

Christian spiritual formation invites us to submit to the work of the Holy Spirit so that we become people of love, joy, peace, and Christlike maturity, people who reflect the beauty and truth of the gospel in every area of life.

Reflection #2: *Have you experienced spiritual transformation before?*

Think of a moment when you felt God reshaping you through joy, pain, Scripture, silence, or community. What changed in you? What stayed with you?

The Framework for the Journey

In this book, we'll explore Christian spiritual formation through the lens of four vital relationships:

- *With God:* where we learn intimacy, trust, and obedience
- *With Others*: where love, forgiveness, and humility are cultivated
- *With Self:* where identity, healing, and integrity are formed
- *With Creation:* where we learn stewardship, rest, and wonder

Each section will include biblical teaching, personal reflection, and time-tested Christian practices that help us grow in grace and truth.

Reflection #3: *What do you hunger for in this season?*

Is there a longing in your heart right now for peace, healing, purpose, clarity, or deeper intimacy with God?

The Call to Be Transformed

This journey won't be easy or instant. There will be resistance from within and without. But spiritual formation is not about striving to earn

God's love; it's about living from the love you've already been given.

Christian spiritual formation is ultimately not something we accomplish, but something God accomplishes in us as we yield to Him day by day (Philippians 1:6).

Reflection #4: *Are you willing to be shaped?*

Formation requires more than curiosity; it requires surrender. What might God be asking you to release so He can begin reshaping your heart?

So if you're still here, still reading, then I believe the Spirit is calling you. Not to become a religious perfectionist, but to become someone more fully alive in Christ. Someone shaped by truth, love, and grace. Someone formed by the Spirit.

Take a deep breath. Turn the page. Let the journey begin.

Section I
Relationship with God

Chapter 1
Knowing the Triune God

I did not grow up thinking much about the Trinity. I heard the words "Father, Son, and Holy Spirit" spoken at baptisms, recited in prayers, or sung in doxologies, but they often felt like a formal introduction to a God I barely knew. It wasn't until years later, sitting in a quiet chapel with the sunlight falling across an open Bible, that I began to sense there was more.

The passage I was reading was John 17, where Jesus prays for His followers. But it was this line that captured me: "As you, Father, are in me and I am in you, may they also be in us" (John 17:21). In that moment, it dawned on me: Jesus wasn't just describing a theological idea. He was revealing a relationship which was so deep, so mutual, and so loving that it overflowed into the world. This is where Christian spiritual formation begins. Not with what we do, but with who God is a Triune God, eternal communion, endless love.

The Triune God
A Divine Communion of Love

The Scriptures describe God not as a solitary monologue but as a living communion. Throughout the New Testament, the relationship among Creator, Christ, and Spirit unfolds like a conversation of love. Jesus says, "I am in the Father and the Father is in me" (John 14:10–11), and later promises the Spirit "who comes from the Father" and "testifies" about Christ (John 15:26). Here is a picture of God that is vibrant, relational, and interconnected.

The early Christian theologians (especially the Cappadocian Fathers like Basil the Great, Gregory of Nyssa, Gregory of Nazianzus) used the word *perichoresis* to describe this divine relationship. *Perichoresis* means "mutual indwelling," "interpenetration," or "a divine dance." It expresses the idea that the persons of the Trinity share life completely while retaining their distinct personhood.

Later thinkers like Jurgen Moltmann and Miroslav Volf expanded this into what is called the social Trinitarian view: that God's very being is relationship, and therefore human beings who are made in God's image are created for relationship. To know God as Trinity is to see God as loving communion.

Reflection #1: *How does imagining God as a loving communion, rather than a distant figure, shape your sense of God's heart?*

Formation Begins with Participation

Christian spiritual formation is not simply self-improvement with religious language. It is participation in the very life of God.

Paul describes salvation as being "hidden with Christ in God" (Colossians 3:3) and tells believers, "It is Christ who lives in you" (Galatians

2:20). Through the Holy Spirit, we are welcomed into the divine relationship: "You have received the Spirit of adoption... the Spirit testifies with our spirit that we are God's children" (Romans 8:15–16).

The entire spiritual life flows from this shared life with God.

- *We pray* because the Spirit prompts us (Romans 8:26).
- *We love* because Christ first loved us (1 John 4:19).
- *We grow* because the Creator is shaping us (Ephesians 2:10).

Spiritual formation begins not in effort but in union, in dwelling with God, and participating in divine love.

Reflection #2: *When you think about your spiritual growth, do you imagine it as something you must do alone, or something God is inviting you into?*

Perichoresis and the Shape of Human Community

If God's life is mutual, loving, and interdependent, then the Christian life cannot be individualistic.

The social Trinity suggests that the way God relates is the model for how humans are meant to relate with dignity, compassion, reciprocity, and unity-in-diversity. Paul uses the metaphor of the body to describe the church: "Just as the body is one and has many members… so it is with Christ" (1 Corinthians 12:12).

In other words, we don't simply believe in community; we were designed from the beginning to live in it because God is community. Miroslav Volf writes, "Because the Christian God is a community of persons in the unity of love, God's followers must live in community that mirrors God's inner life." To be spiritually formed is to become more relational, not less, but more connected, more reconciled, more compassionate.

Reflection #3: *Where in your life do you experience genuine mutuality, relationships marked by shared love and shared life? Where do you hunger for more of this?*

Knowing the Trinity Through Experience

The Trinity may be mysterious, but the Bible never presents God as inaccessible. We come to know the Triune God not only through doctrine but through experience:

The Creator is encountered in the beauty and order of creation (Psalm 19:1), in breath and life itself (Genesis 2:7).

Christ is encountered in Scripture (John 1:14), in compassion and justice (Luke 4:18–19), and in the call to discipleship (Mark 1:17).

The Spirit is encountered in guidance (John 16:13), empowerment (Acts 1:8), comfort (John 14:26), and inner transformation (2 Corinthians 3:18).

Throughout Christian history, mystics like Augustine, Julian of Norwich, and Teresa of Ávila consistently describe encountering God in ways that reflect Trinity-shaped intimacy, that is, God beyond us, with us, and within us. Spiritual formation invites us to attend to these encounters, to become aware of God's presence in all things.

Reflection #4: *Which person of the Trinity (Creator, Christ, or Spirit) feels closest to you right now? Which may be inviting you into deeper relationship?*

The Invitation to the Dance

If *perichoresis* describes the mutual indwelling of the Triune God, then Jesus' prayer in John 17 reveals something astonishing: we are invited into the dance, not as spectators and not as guests, but as participants. We are welcomed into the shared life of God.

This is the foundation of Christian spiritual formation: God forming us from within God's own love. As Paul proclaims, "In God we live and move and have our being" (Acts 17:28). Our transformation flows from the One who created us, redeemed us, and dwells within us. So the journey begins here in the embrace of the Triune God who has always known you, always loved you, and always desired communion with you.

Take a breath. Enter the mystery. You are being invited into the divine life.

Chapter 2
Prayer and the Presence

There was a time when I thought prayer was something I had to do right to make God pay attention. I treated it like leaving a voicemail on heaven's answering machine, hoping I said the right words, used the right tone, maybe even impressed God a little.

But then I began to discover something far more beautiful: Prayer is not performance. It is participation. Prayer is not about waking God up; it is about waking myself up to the God who is already here.

Prayer as Relational Presence

In the Christian tradition, prayer is not a monologue but a conversation, not a task but a relationship. The psalmist cries out: "You search out my path and my lying down, and are acquainted with all my ways… Where can I go from your Spirit? Or where can I flee from your presence?" (Psalm 139:3, 7).

This awareness that God is always present is the foundation of a prayerful life. We are not summoning a distant deity. We are turning toward the One who is already near, already listening, already loving.

Jesus models this kind of relational prayer in His own life. Time and again, we see Him withdrawing to pray, not because He lacked power, but because He craved communion. "But Jesus often withdrew to lonely places and prayed" (Luke 5:16). In John 11:41–42, before raising Lazarus, He begins His prayer, "Father, I thank you that you have heard me. I knew that you always hear me." Prayer, for Jesus, is not a ritual. It is ongoing relationship with the One He calls "Abba."

The Witness of the Ancients
Desert Wisdom and Contemplation

From the earliest days of the church, prayer was seen as the soul's lifeline to God, not just intercession, but transformation.

John Cassian, a fifth-century monk who recorded the wisdom of the Desert Fathers, taught that the aim of prayer was not eloquence but pure attention to God. "Prayer," he wrote, "is the raising of the heart and mind to God."

Evagrius Ponticus, another desert theologian, famously said, "If you are a theologian, you will pray truly. And if you pray truly, you are a theologian." Prayer wasn't separate from theology; it was theology embodied. Syncletica of Alexandria, a desert mother, taught that silence and stillness were the gateway to divine presence: "There are many who live in the desert, yet behave as if they were in the town. It is better to be in the town and keep peace within than to be in the desert and inwardly in conflict."

Prayer begins not with geography, but with attention.

Reflection #1: *What assumptions about prayer have shaped your practice? Has prayer felt like a task, a transaction, or a place of presence?*

Prayer as Formation, Not Performance

Jesus' disciples didn't ask Him how to lead, heal, or preach. They asked, "Lord, teach us to pray" (Luke 11:1).

In response, Jesus gave them the Lord's Prayer (Matthew 6:9–13), a prayer that orients the soul toward God, community, daily needs, forgiveness, and freedom. Each phrase is deeply relational and formational.

- *"Our Creator in heaven"* Intimacy with transcendence.
- *"Your kingdom come"* Alignment with God's vision.
- *"Give us this day…"* Trust in divine provision.
- *"Forgive us…"* Humility and reconciliation.

Prayer does not change God; it changes us.

Reflection #2: *Which line in the Lord's Prayer speaks most powerfully to you right now? Why might that be?*

Practicing the Presence of God

In the 17th century, Brother Lawrence, a Carmelite monk, revolutionized prayer not by preaching sermons, but by washing dishes. In *The Practice of the Presence of God,* he wrote: "There is not in the world a kind of life more sweet and delightful than that of a continual conversation with God."

Brother Lawrence discovered that every act (e.g., cleaning, cooking, walking) could be a prayer, if it was done in loving awareness of God's presence.

This is the invitation of attentive prayer: not to escape the world, but to find God in it.

The Spirit Helps Us Pray

Even when we lack words, the Spirit prays within us. Paul writes: "The Spirit helps us in our weakness… with sighs too deep for words" (Romans 8:26).

The Spirit is not an outside force; the Spirit is God's presence within, interceding, comforting, forming. Even silence becomes prayer when offered in trust.

Reflection #3: *When has the Spirit prayed through your silence, your grief, and your joy even when words failed?*

Conclusion

Prayer as a Place to Dwell

Prayer is not an escape; it is a return. It brings us home to God, to ourselves, and to one another.

Julian of Norwich, the 14th-century mystic, wrote: "Prayer unites the soul to God… for by prayer, the soul is made pliable and gentle." To be spiritually formed through prayer is to become more attuned to God's presence, to the rhythms of grace, and to the needs of the world.

Reflection #4: *What part of your life is God inviting into prayerful awareness of your work, your relationships, your rest, even your pain?*

Prayer Practice Guide

1. Cultivating Presence

The following exercises are designed to help you move from learning about prayer to living prayerfully, engaging the presence of God in ordinary life. Choose one to begin with. Don't rush. Let each practice become a way of being with God, not just doing something for God.

Breath Prayer (Prayer in Every Moment)

Purpose

To help you connect with God throughout your day using your body and breath.

How it works

Breath prayer is a short, sacred phrase synchronized with your breathing. It anchors your attention in God's presence, calms anxiety, and draws your awareness back to divine love in the moment.

Practice

Sit comfortably or stand still. Close your eyes if you feel safe to do so. Begin breathing slowly and deeply. Choose a phrase that speaks to your current need. Examples:

- *Inhale: Jesus… | Exhale: Be my peace.*
- *Inhale: Abba… | Exhale: I belong to You.*
- *Inhale: Spirit… | Exhale: Lead me in love.*

Repeat the phrase gently with your breath for 3–5 minutes. When distractions come, gently return to the breath and the phrase.

Time

3–5 minutes (or throughout the day)

Scriptural Root

Psalm 46:10: "Be still, and know that I am God."

2. The Daily *Examen*
Reflective Prayer with God

Purpose

To reflect prayerfully on your day, discern God's presence, and grow in awareness.

How it works

The *Examen*, adapted from St. Ignatius of Loyola, is a simple method of reviewing your day with God, noticing where grace appeared, where growth is needed, and where peace can be received.

Practice (Evening or End of Day)

- *Become aware of God's presence.* Invite the Spirit to guide your memory and attention.
- *Review the day with gratitude.* What are you thankful for? Name even small things.

- *Pay attention to emotions.* Where were you anxious, joyful, angry, or peaceful?
- *Choose one moment.* Let it become a conversation with God; ask questions, listen, respond.
- *Look forward with hope.* Ask for God's grace for the next day.

Time

10–15 minutes

Scriptural Root

Psalm 139:23–24 "Search me, O God, and know my heart…"

3. Centering Prayer
Silent Union with God

Purpose

To move beyond words into silence and resting presence with God.

How it works

Centering Prayer teaches you to sit in silence, consenting to God's presence and action within you. It's not about thinking or achieving; it's about being.

Practice

- *Find a quiet place.* Set a timer for 10–20 minutes.
- *Sit in a relaxed but upright position.*

- *Choose a sacred word* (e.g., Peace, Love, *Abba*, Jesus) as a symbol of your desire to be with God.
- *Silently repeat this word* when you notice your thoughts wandering.
- *At the end, gently return from the silence* and offer a short prayer of thanks.

Time

10–20 minutes (start with 5–10 if new)

Scriptural Root

1 Kings 19:12 "And after the fire came a gentle whisper..."

4. *Lectio Divina*
Praying with Scripture

Purpose

To hear God through Scripture in a personal, relational way.

How it works

Lectio Divina (Latin for "sacred reading") is a slow, meditative way of encountering God through the Word with your heart, not just your head.

Practice

- *Prepare:* Choose a short Scripture (e.g., Psalm 23, John 15:1–8). Sit quietly and invite the Spirit to speak.
- *Read (Lectio)*: Read the passage slowly and aloud if possible.

- *Reflect* (*Meditatio*): What word or phrase stands out to you? Sit with it. Repeat it.
- *Respond* (*Oratio*): Speak to God from what you noticed. Be honest. Be simple.
- *Rest* (*Contemplatio*): Let go of words. Rest in God's presence. Be still.

Time

15–20 minutes

Scriptural Root

Hebrews 4:12 "The word of God is living and active…"

Final Encouragement

Don't aim for perfection. Don't wait to feel "spiritual." These practices are not for professionals; they are for pilgrims. They are paths, not performances.

Start small. Be consistent. Trust the Spirit to do the work of formation in hidden, gentle ways.

Chapter 3
Scripture as Sacred Encounter and Formation

I used to read the Bible to find answers.

It was a habit formed early, turning to Scripture when I needed comfort, clarity, or certainty. I'd flip through passages like a spiritual search engine, hoping for insight or guidance. I treated the Word of God as if it contained data to download, something I could master, quote, or explain.

But over time, something deeper began to stir. I noticed how often the words spoke to me before I ever had a chance to speak about them. Scripture began to confront me, comfort me, uncover my hidden motives, and rewire my view of God and myself.

I realized the Bible wasn't just a book to understand it was a space to inhabit. A voice to listen to, a presence to enter. That's when Scripture became sacred encounter, not just information but transformation.

Scripture as More Than Information

This shift from reading the Bible as a source of content to encountering it as a means of formation is a vital one. As Jesus told the religious experts of His day: "You search the Scriptures because you think that in them you have eternal life; and it is they that testify about me. Yet you refuse to come to me to have life" (John 5:39–40). They had the text, but missed the Person.

They studied Scripture but failed to be shaped by it. They treated it as a manual for control rather than an invitation into communion. Scripture, when rightly approached, doesn't just give us facts. It forms our desires, awakens our conscience, shapes our imagination, and draws us deeper into the life of God.

Scripture as Formation

Mark A. Maddix and Richard P. Thompson articulate this beautifully in their work, *Scripture as Formation*. They suggest that Scripture's primary function in the church is not to merely transmit information, but to form people into the image of Christ.

According to their research:

- *Scripture is meant to shape hearts, not just fill minds.*
- *The authority of Scripture is demonstrated not only in its content but in its capacity to transform individuals and communities.*
- *True biblical interpretation must be communal, spiritual, and experiential, not just analytical or intellectual.*

They remind us that the early church didn't view Scripture as an academic document to be dissected, but as a sacred source of life and transformation, often read aloud in worship, interpreted together, and practiced in community.

Scripture Becomes Scripture in Community

Scripture comes fully alive not just in solitude, but in the gathered community of worship. Ezra read the Torah aloud to the people, "so that all the people could hear and understand" (Nehemiah 8:3). Jesus read from the scroll of Isaiah in the synagogue, and said, "Today this Scripture has been fulfilled in your hearing" (Luke 4:21). Paul expected his letters to be read aloud "to all the brothers and sisters" (1 Thessalonians 5:27).

Maddix and Thompson affirm this: Scripture becomes Scripture in the life of the church, not in isolation, but in worship, dialogue, mutual correction, and shared obedience. In that space, the Word becomes not just a book, but a formative encounter with God.

Reading to Be Formed, Not Just Informed

When we approach Scripture as formational, we do more than study it. We let it study us. "For the word of God is living and active… it judges the thoughts and intentions of the heart" (Hebrews 4:12). This Word is not passive. It speaks. It cuts. It heals. It reshapes who we are and how we live. It is God-breathed (2 Timothy 3:16), and its purpose is to train us in righteousness and make us whole.

The early church practiced this through *Lectio Divina*, the slow, sacred reading where Scripture becomes prayer.

- *Communal reading* where interpretation was shaped by the Spirit and the gathered Body.

- *Confession and application* where the Word was not finished until it was lived.

Scripture Shapes Identity and Mission

Because Scripture is God's story, it shapes our story. We are not orphans; we are image-bearers (Genesis 1:27). We are not aimless; we are a chosen people (1 Peter 2:9). We are not condemned; we are a new creation (2 Corinthians 5:17). We are not alone; we are the Body of Christ (Romans 12:5).

As Maddix and Thompson note, Scripture forms us not just as individuals, but as a people with a shared narrative, shared ethics, and a shared mission in the world.

A Rhythm for Sacred Encounter with Scripture

To approach Scripture as formation, try this rhythm in personal or communal settings:

- *Prepare.* Sit in silence. Breathe deeply. Ask the Holy Spirit to guide you.
- *Read Slowly.* Choose a short passage. Read it aloud. Let it speak.
- *Listen Attentively.* Notice what stirs: a word, phrase, image, or emotion. Don't rush to analyze. Just notice.
- *Respond Prayerfully.* Speak with God. Express what the Word awakened in you. Confess. Ask. Thank.
- *Rest in God's Presence.* Let the Word dwell in you richly (Colossians 3:16). Be still.

- *Live the Word.* Ask: How will this Word shape my actions, relationships, priorities today?
- *Return Together.* Read and reflect in community. Let others' voices deepen your understanding. Let the Spirit guide the Body.

Conclusion
Let the Word Form You

Scripture is not just an ancient document. It is a living voice. A sacred space. A transformative power.

When we read it in solitude and community, not just for information but for formation, it becomes what it was always meant to be: a means of grace. A wellspring of life. The very breath of God. As Maddix and Thompson remind us: we don't master Scripture. We are mastered by it, lovingly, until we become more like Christ.

So come to the Word. Not to study it, but to dwell in it. To let it dwell in you. And to let it form the people of God. "Let the word of Christ dwell in you richly, as you teach and admonish one another with all wisdom…" (Colossians 3:16).

Chapter 4
Worship as Transformation
Word, Table, and True Orthodoxy

When I was younger, I thought being "orthodox" simply meant having the right beliefs the right cree, and the right doctrines. I memorized statements of faith, learned theological truths, argued about what's correct. But somewhere along the way, I began to sense something more profound: true orthodoxy is not just about "right doctrine," but about right worship, worship that aligns us with God, forms our hearts, and transforms our lives.

In fact, the very word "orthodoxy" in Greek (*orthos,* straight, right plus *doxa,* glory, worship, praise) carries both meanings: "right belief" and "right worship. That means authentic Christian orthodoxy is as much about how we worship God as about what we believe.

Worship is not secondary to theology. Worship is where theology becomes life. Worship is where God meets us. Worship is where we are transformed both as individuals and as community.

Why Worship Matters
Orthodoxy in Practice, Not Just Theory

Over many centuries, the church has often defined "orthodoxy" in terms of doctrinal agreement: the correct understanding of God, Christ, the Trinity, salvation, Scripture. Those are vital. But if orthodoxy remains only in our heads, it risks becoming cold, empty, lifeless.

True orthodoxy, hearing the right words and worshiping with the right heart, always leads to orthopraxy (right practice) or, more precisely, right worship. In many Christian traditions, especially in the early church and among Eastern believers, worship is considered central: not optional, not decorative, but foundational.

Worship is the place where heaven and earth meet. The Word of God is proclaimed, the Table is set. Believers enter the mystery of God's presence. In worship, theology becomes doxology. True understanding becomes true praise. And the church is formed as the Body of Christ.

The Ancient Shape of Worship
Word + Table + Communion + Mission

From the earliest days, Christian worship has followed a pattern that reflects both belief and devotion, doctrine and doxology. That shape can be summarized:

- *Gathering:* believers come together, acknowledging that faith is not private but communal.
- *Proclamation of the Word:* reading, preaching, hearing Scripture. The Word of God is heard, proclaimed, received.
- *Table (Eucharist/Communion):* sharing bread and cup, remembering Christ's death and

resurrection, participating in His body and blood.

- *Sending (Mission & Life):* being sent into the world to live what worship has shaped in us.

This pattern isn't a human invention; it arises from Gospel reality and early church tradition. Worship thus becomes not only a Sunday ritual, but a means of formation, identity, and mission.

The Word
Hearing God, Being Formed

When we gather for worship, we don't start with our own words. God speaks first. The proclamation of Scripture, the reading of the Word, is central. In the earliest Christian communities, believers devoted themselves to "the apostles' teaching and to fellowship, to the breaking of bread and to prayer." (Acts 2:42)

Proclamation of God's Word isn't an academic lecture; it's a spiritual encounter. As believers, when we listen, we invite God to transform us: to convict, to comfort, to reorient, to call. The Word shapes our theology, but more importantly, it shapes our hearts and lives. Right worship begins here: in hearing God rightly.

The Table
Participation, Communion, Transformation

But the Word alone isn't enough. The Table (Communion, Eucharist, the Lord's Supper, Mass) is where Word becomes flesh (as it always has), where memory becomes presence, where we as a gathered people participate in Christ's death and resurrection.

Through the Table, we remember the cross, we proclaim the resurrection, and we are incorporated into the Body. Communion is identity: we are not spectators; we are participants. To partake is to declare that the Gospel isn't theory; it's life. The Table calls us into unity, humility, love, and mission. When we worship at Table, orthodoxy becomes communal, not just "my belief," but "our belonging."

Worship as Orthodox Life
Doxology, Doctrine, and Daily Living

Because orthodoxy means right worship, worship is not limited to Sunday or to a building. The pattern of worship spills over into every facet of life, work, rest, justice, relationships, service, creation care, mission. True worship forms us into a people whose lives reflect the values of Christ: compassion, humility, generosity, holiness. The worship we offer corporately becomes the prism through which we view daily life. In this way, orthodoxy becomes living: theology becomes doxology becomes praxis; right worship becomes right living.

What Worship Does
Transformation, Identity, Community, Mission
Formation of Heart and Soul

In worship, God shapes us. Through Word and Table, we are reminded who God is and who we are. We are formed not just in mind, but in spirit, will, and love.

Formation of Community

Worship unites people from different backgrounds, experiences, struggles, and hopes into one Body. At the Table, we share one bread, one cup; in the Word, we hear one voice. Worship creates and shapes identity: we belong together.

Formation of Mission and Purpose

Worship doesn't end with the benediction. We leave worship "sent" to live out God's love, justice, mercy, reconciliation, stewardship, hope. Worship becomes commissioning for life beyond the walls.

Reflection

What Does Orthodoxy (Right Worship) Mean for You?

Do you see worship as just a Sunday obligation or as a formative meeting with God?

When Scripture is read aloud and preached, does your heart respond, not merely with knowledge, but with worship?

In Communion, do you sense belonging to the Body of Christ, not just individuals, but a community sharing life, forgiveness, and hope?

Does worship shape your daily life, your relationships, your choices, and your mission? Or does it stay contained in church walls and weekly routines?

Conclusion
Worship as Orthodoxy in Action

If orthodoxy, true faith, is about right worship as much as right belief, then worship is not a "nice add-on." Worship is fundamental. Worship is formative. Worship is transformative.

When we gather, hear the Word, share the Table, respond in love, and go out to serve, we are living out orthodoxy. We are being transformed. We are becoming more of what God created us to be. So come to worship not simply to hear or sing, but come to be formed. Come to know the living God, as we meet Him in Word and table, as a body, as a people, as a movement of grace into the world.

Section II
Relationship with Others

Chapter 5
The Body of Christ
Being Formed in Community

The Christian life begins not with an individual confession but with a communal summons. When Jesus teaches His disciples to pray, He does not say, "My Father," but "Our Father" (Matthew 6:9). Before a believer ever speaks alone in private devotion, he or she is gathered into a shared identity. The grammar of the gospel is plural. Spiritual formation, therefore, cannot be reduced to the shaping of private piety. It is the Spirit's work of forming a people—a living body—into the likeness of Christ. To understand this, we must begin where Scripture begins.

Created in the Image of Communion

Genesis opens with a God who speaks in plurality: "Let us make man in our image" (Genesis 1:26). Whatever mysteries surround that divine "us," the New Testament reveals its fullness in the triune life of Father, Son, and Spirit (Matthew 28:19; 2 Corinthians 13:14). God is not solitary. God is communion.

Humanity, made in this image, is created for relational life. Before sin fractures the world, God declares, "It is not good that the man should be alone" (Genesis 2:18). Isolation is named as a deficiency in an otherwise unfallen creation. From the beginning, spiritual flourishing is tied to relational belonging.

Sin, in turn, fractures communion—first with God (Genesis 3:8–10), then with one another (Genesis 4:8). The story of redemption is therefore the story of restored relationship. God does not merely rescue individuals; He reconstitutes a people.

A Covenant People

When God calls Abram, the promise is communal: "I will make of you a great nation" (Genesis 12:2). At Sinai, Israel is formed as "a kingdom of priests and a holy nation" (Exodus 19:6). The covenant is not given to scattered individuals but to an assembled people.

The law shapes communal life—care for the poor (Deuteronomy 15), shared feasts (Leviticus 23), justice in courts (Deuteronomy 16), rhythms of Sabbath rest for all (Exodus 20:8–11). Holiness is social before it is private. The prophets continue this emphasis. Isaiah rebukes Israel not merely for personal immorality but for communal injustice (Isaiah 1:16–17). Amos con-demns worship divorced from social righteousness (Amos 5:21–24). God's concern is always the shape of the people together.

By the time we reach Ezekiel, the promise of renewal is explicitly corporate: "I will give you a new heart… and I will put my Spirit within you" (Ezekiel 36:26–27). The Spirit's coming will create a transformed community.

Jesus' Ministry

When Jesus begins His ministry, He does not gather isolated followers for private enlightenment. He calls twelve (Mark 3:13–19), symbolically reconstituting Israel. He forms a visible community around Himself.

He gives them a new commandment: "Love one another: just as I have loved you" (John 13:34). The mark of discipleship is not merely doctrinal precision but embodied love: "By this all people will know that you are my disciples" (13:35).

In John 17, Jesus prays not only for the Twelve but "for those who will believe in me through their word, that they may all be one… so that the world may believe that you have sent me" (John 17:20–21). Unity is not optional; it is missional.

The cross itself creates community. Paul declares that Christ "has broken down in his flesh the dividing wall of hostility… that he might create in himself one new humanity" (Ephesians 2:14–15). Jew and Gentile—once separated—are reconciled "in one body through the cross" (2:16).

The church is not a religious association. It is a new humanity.

The Church as the Body of Christ

Paul's language intensifies in 1 Corinthians 12: "For just as the body is one and has many members… so it is with Christ. For in one Spirit we were all baptized into one body" (12:12–13). Notice the radical claim: the church is not merely like Christ's body—it is Christ's body. Union with

Christ produces union with one another. "The eye cannot say to the hand, 'I have no need of you'" (12:21).

Spiritual gifts are given "for the common good" (12:7). Maturity is not measured by private spiritual experience but by mutual edification. When one suffers, all suffer (12:26). Interdependence is not weakness; it is design.

Ephesians expands the vision: Christ "gave... apostles, prophets, evangelists, shepherds and teachers, to equip the saints... for building up the body of Christ, until we all attain... mature manhood" (Ephesians 4:11–13). Growth is corporate. The body "builds itself up in love" as each part functions properly (4:16). Formation is coordinated growth in communion.

The Practices of the Early Church

The earliest believers lived this truth. In the book of Acts, the church devoted itself not just to doctrine, but to life together in teaching, fellowship, prayer, and breaking bread (Acts 2:42). That radical koinonia shaped Christian identity. It challenged isolation. It nurtured belonging. It formed disciples.

They shared possessions so "there was not a needy person among them" (Acts 4:34). Their fellowship had economic consequences. They met in homes. They ate with "glad and generous hearts." Their life together was visible and compelling.

The writer of Hebrews later exhorts believers: "Let us consider how to stir up one another to love and good works, not neglecting to meet together" (Hebrews 10:24–25). Community requires intentional gathering and mutual exhortation. James commands, "Confess your sins to one another and pray for one another, that you may be healed" (James 5:16). Healing is communal.

The New Testament vision is unmistakable: believers are formed through shared worship, shared confession, shared mission, and shared suffering.

Practices That Shape the Body Today

If Scripture provides the theological foundation, the question becomes practical: How is this communal formation cultivated in the contemporary church?

Recovering the Table

From Passover (Exodus 12) to the Lord's Supper (1 Corinthians 11:23–26) to the Marriage Supper of the Lamb (Revelation 19:9), redemption is tasted as well as proclaimed. Shared meals embody welcome. The Eucharist proclaims unity. Ordinary hospitality extends sacramental grace into daily life. When churches foster rhythms of table fellowship—across socioeconomic and generational lines—they make visible the reconciling work of Christ.

Smaller Communities Within the Larger Assembly

The early believers gathered in both temple courts and homes (Acts 2:46). Large assemblies proclaim; smaller gatherings transform. In intimate spaces, believers confess sin, wrestle with Scripture, discern gifts, and intercede specifically. Without such contexts, churches risk producing attenders rather than disciples.

Intergenerational Formation

Paul instructs older men and women to teach younger believers (Titus 2:1–8). Faith is transmitted through a relationship. When generations share life, wisdom tempers zeal, and zeal revives wisdom. The church becomes a living memory of God's faithfulness.

Covenant Commitment

Romans 12:5 declares, "We, though many, are one body in Christ, and individually members one of another." Membership is not a consumer choice but a covenant belonging. Teaching the seriousness of belonging—mutual care, accountability, perseverance—cultivates stability in an age of preference-driven mobility.

Shared Mission

Jesus sends His disciples as the Father sent Him (John 20:21). The church discovers unity in shared obedience. Serving the poor, welcoming the stranger, pursuing justice—these are not peripheral activities but formative practices. Working side by side shapes hearts and bonds believers together.

Repentance and Reconciliation

If Christ reconciled us to God and entrusted us with the ministry of reconciliation (2 Corinthians

5:18), then forgiveness must be habitual in the church. Conflict handled with humility strengthens the community. Repentance modeled publicly creates safety. A reconciled people reflects a crucified Savior.

The Witness of a Formed Community

Jesus' prayer remains: "That they may all be one... so that the world may believe" (John 17:21). The credibility of the gospel is intertwined with the visible love of the church. In a fragmented world, a unified community becomes a sign of divine life.

Spiritual formation in community is slow and ordinary. It unfolds in shared meals and shared tears, in confession and communion, in service and reconciliation. Over time, a people emerges who resemble their Lord. We do not create this unity. The Spirit has already made us one body. Our task is to grow into what we already are.

Reflection Questions

How does the doctrine of the Trinity shape my understanding of Christian community?

In what ways does my church reflect (or resist) the New Testament vision of shared life?

Where am I practicing meaningful and profound interdependence rather than spiritual independence?

How does our congregation embody covenant commitment over consumer preference?

What practices in our community most visibly display reconciliation and unity?

If our shared life were the primary evidence for the gospel, what would it communicate

Selected Bibliography

Dietrich Bonhoeffer, *Life Together* (Orbis Books, 1998).

Stanley Hauerwas, *A Community of Character* (University of Notre Dame Press, 1981).

Christine Pohl, *Making Room* (Eerdmans, 2024).

Jean Vanier, *Community and Growth* (Paulist Press, 1979).

John Zizioulas, *Being as Communion* (St. Vladimir's Seminary Press, 1985).

Chapter 6
Living Reconciliation
Justice, Compassion, and Hospitality

At the center of the Christian faith stands not an idea, but a crucified and risen Lord. And at the center of the cross stands reconciliation. The gospel announces that what was fractured has been restored, what was alienated has been brought near, and what was hostile has been made peace. But reconciliation is not merely a doctrine to affirm; it is a life to inhabit. Spiritual formation is the slow shaping of persons and communities who embody the reconciling heart of God in a wounded world.

To speak of reconciliation is to speak of justice, compassion, and hospitality—because these are not peripheral concerns in Scripture. They arise from the very character of God.

The God Who Makes Peace

The biblical story opens with shalom: humanity living in communion with God, one another, and creation. Sin fractures that communion. Adam and Eve hide from God (Genesis 3:8). Blame replaces trust. Soon Cain kills Abel, and alienation spills into violence (Genesis 4:8). The rest of Scripture unfolds as God's relentless pursuit of restoration.

When Joseph stands before the brothers who betrayed him, he declares, "You meant evil against me, but God meant it for good" (Genesis 50:20). His forgiveness does not deny injustice; it transforms it. Joseph becomes a living sign of reconciliation grounded in trust in God's providence.

In 2 Samuel 9, King David seeks out Mephibosheth, the disabled grandson of Saul—his former enemy—and restores him to the king's table. This act of covenant mercy mirrors God's steadfast love. Justice and compassion converge not in punishment, but in restoration.

The prophets press this theme further. When Israel's worship becomes hollow, Amos thunders, "Let justice roll down like waters" (Amos 5:24). Isaiah insists that true fasting involves loosening the bonds of wickedness and sharing bread with the hungry (Isaiah 58:6–7). Justice is not an optional social concern; it is covenanting fidelity embodied.

The rest of Scripture tells the story of a God who refuses to abandon His creation to fragmentation. When Paul writes, "In Christ God was reconciling the world to himself" (2 Corinthians 5:19), he is naming the climax of that long story. Reconciliation begins in God's initiative. "While we were enemies, we were reconciled to God by the death of his Son" (Romans 5:10). The cross does not merely forgive; it restores relationship. It absorbs hostility and establishes peace.

But the gospel moves outward. Those reconciled to God are given "the ministry of reconciliation" (2 Corinthians 5:18). The church becomes a reconciled and reconciling people. This reconciliation is not sentimental harmony. It is costly peace.

Ephesians makes this clear. Christ "is our peace," Paul writes, "who has made both one and has broken down in his flesh the dividing wall of hostility" (Ephesians 2:14). Jew and Gentile—divided by history, theology, and suspicion—are made "one new humanity." The cross creates a new social reality. Reconciliation with God necessarily reshapes human relationships.

Justice in the Character of God

If reconciliation reveals God's mercy, justice reveals His righteousness. "Righteousness and justice are the foundation of your throne," declares Psalm 89:14. God does not merely love justice; justice is woven into His reign. In Scripture, justice is not abstract fairness. It is covenant faithfulness expressed in concrete action—protecting the vulnerable, defending the poor, confronting oppression.

Again, the prophets warn Israel that worship without justice is empty. "Let justice roll down like waters," Amos cries (Amos 5:24). Isaiah rebukes fasting that ignores the hungry and oppressed (Isaiah 58). The measure of fidelity to God is found not only in liturgy but in love enacted toward neighbor.

Jesus stands squarely in this prophetic tradition. He announces good news to the poor, freedom for captives, and release for the oppressed (Luke 4:18–19). He touches lepers, eats with sinners, dignifies women, and restores outcasts. His miracles are not displays of raw power but signs of restored order—glimpses of the kingdom where justice and mercy meet.

At the cross, justice and mercy are united. Sin is not dismissed; it is judged. Yet that judgment falls upon Christ Himself. God remains just while justifying the ungodly (Romans 3:26). Justice is satisfied, and mercy triumphs.

To be conformed to Christ, then, is to become a person in whom justice and compassion are no longer rivals.

A Formed People of Reconciliation

Spiritual formation trains believers to live from the cross outward. Reconciliation begins with confession. A community that names its sins—pride, prejudice, indifference, greed—becomes capable of grace. Confession dismantles the illusion of moral superiority. It creates space for truth and healing. "Confess your sins to one another," James writes, "and pray for one another, that you may be healed" (James 5:16).

Lament follows confession. The Psalms teach God's people to grieve injustice without losing hope. Lament refuses to normalize suffering. It gives voice to victims and keeps the heart tender. A church that cannot lament will soon become numb.

Hospitality extends reconciliation into ordinary life. Israel was commanded to love the stranger, remembering its own story of exile (Deuteronomy 10:19). Jesus identifies Himself with the stranger in Matthew 25. To welcome the outsider is to welcome Christ. Shared tables break down suspicion. They make peace visible.

Generosity reshapes economic life. The early believers shared their possessions so that none lacked (Acts 4:34). Justice is not merely sentiment; it has material consequences. The way a community handles resources reveals what it believes about love.

Peacemaking completes the picture. Jesus calls His followers "peacemakers" (Matthew 5:9). This requires courage. It means confronting sin, pursuing forgiveness, and refusing to allow resentment to calcify into division. In a culture addicted to outrage and avoidance, peacemaking is revolutionary.

These practices form persons who are capable of reconciliation. But they are not ends in themselves. They prepare the church to engage the world.

The Early Church
A Formed Community of Justice and Mercy

The book of Acts offers more than theological claims; it shows reconciliation embodied. In Acts 6, a dispute arises between Hellenistic and Hebraic Jews over the neglect of widows in food distribution. The apostles do not dismiss the complaint as divisive. They address it structurally, appointing Spirit-filled leaders to ensure equitable care. Justice becomes an expression of spiritual maturity.

Acts 11 describes believers in Antioch sending relief to famine-stricken Judea. Ethnic and geographic boundaries are crossed in tangible solidarity. Generosity flows from shared identity in Christ.

The early church fathers continued this pattern. During the plagues of the second and third centuries, pagan populations often fled cities in fear. Christians, however, became known for staying behind to nurse the sick—both fellow believers and strangers. Dionysius of Alexandria described believers who "visited the sick without thought of danger… drawing upon themselves their neighbors' diseases." Their compassion was not a strategy; it was a formation. They had learned to love as Christ loved.

Tertullian reported that pagans would say of Christians, "See how they love one another." Their communal sharing, care for widows and orphans, and burial of the poor distinguished them in a harsh empire. Justice and mercy were not add-ons to worship. They were its fruit.

Practices That Form Reconciling People

If reconciliation and justice are part of Christlikeness, then they must be cultivated intentionally. Confession trains humility. When believers confess sin—personal prejudice, indifference to suffering, complicity in injustice—they are formed into truthful people. Without confession, justice becomes a self-righteous performance.

Lament trains compassion. The Psalms give language for grieving violence and oppression

(Psalm 10; 82). Lament keeps the heart from hardening. It forms empathy.

Hospitality trains love across difference. The command to love the stranger (Deuteronomy 10:19) is repeated in the New Testament (Hebrews 13:2). Shared tables reshape fear into fellowship. They dismantle abstract stereotypes through embodied presence.

Generosity trains detachment from possessions. Acts 4:34 notes that "there was not a needy person among them." Economic life became part of spiritual formation. Giving is not fundraising; it is discipleship.

Peacemaking trains courage. Jesus instructs believers to pursue reconciliation actively (Matthew 5:23–24; 18:15–20). Conflict is not avoided but redeemed. Forgiveness becomes habitual.

These practices shape the heart so that justice in the world is not reactive outrage but steady faithfulness.

Justice as Public Witness

Spiritual formation that remains private is incomplete. The reconciling work of Christ extends into public life. Micah 6:8 calls God's people "to do justice, and to love kindness, and to walk humbly." Justice is something done, not merely affirmed. Yet it is done humbly aware of our own need for mercy.

The early Christians did not possess political power, but they practiced disruptive compassion. They rescued abandoned infants left to die of exposure. They ransomed captives. They cared for the poor across ethnic lines. They bore witness to a different kingdom.

Today, the church's participation in justice may include advocating for the unborn and the elderly, confronting racial inequity, supporting refugees, resisting human trafficking, mentoring fatherless children, or reforming unjust practices in local communities.

These actions are not political trends; they are spiritual disciplines when rooted in love of neighbor and fidelity to Christ.

When believers step into spaces of suffering, they encounter Christ Himself: "As you did it to one of the least of these... you did it to me" (Matthew 25:40). Justice becomes an arena of communion with God.

Formation Between Cross and Kingdom

We live between what Christ has accomplished and what He will consummate. Colossians 1:20 promises that God will reconcile "all things" through Christ. Yet the world still groans. The church does not usher in the kingdom by force. It embodies signs of the kingdom through faithfulness.

Spiritual formation shapes people who resist injustice without hatred, pursue justice without pride, and practice compassion without despair. It forms communities whose shared life makes the gospel credible. Reconciliation and justice are not distractions from spiritual growth. They are dimensions of it.

To be formed by the Spirit is to love what God loves. To love what God loves is to pursue what God pursues. And what God pursues is the restoration of all things.

Reflection Questions

How do biblical stories of reconciliation (Joseph, David and Mephibosheth, the early church) shape my understanding of justice?

In what ways has my spiritual formation neglected the outward call to reconciliation?

How does my church embody tangible care for the vulnerable?

Where is lament needed in our community?

What concrete practice could deepen my participation in Christ's reconciling mission?

How might justice become not merely an activity, but a habit of the heart?

Suggested Reading

John Perkins, *Let Justice Roll Down* (Regal Books, 1976).

Brenda Salter McNeil, *Roadmap to Reconciliation* (IVP, 2015).

Miroslav Volf, *Exclusion and Embrace* (Abingdon, 1996).

Nicholas Wolterstorff, *Justice: Rights and Wrongs* (Princeton University Press, 2008).

Christopher J. H. Wright, *Old Testament Ethics for the People of God* (IVP, 2004).

Chapter 7
Embodied Witness
Loving Neighbor, Embracing Creation

Spiritual formation is not disembodied. It does not float above the world in private devotion, nor does it culminate in inward serenity alone. The Spirit who forms us into the likeness of Christ does so during soil and sweat, neighborhoods and ecosystems, human need and nonhuman creation. The Christian life is not an escape from the material world but participation in God's redeeming love for it. To be spiritually formed is to become an embodied witness—one who loves neighbor and embraces creation as an expression of communion with God.

Love of neighbor and care for creation are not secondary ethical add-ons. They arise from the very shape of the biblical story and the character of the Triune God.

The Biblical Ground
Love of Neighbor

When asked to name the greatest commandment, Jesus answered with two inseparable loves: "You shall love the Lord your God with all your heart and with all your soul and with all your mind… And a second is like it: You shall love your neighbor as yourself" (Matthew 22:37–39).

Love of God and love of neighbor are not competing priorities. They are mutually interpreting realities. One cannot claim devotion to God while neglecting neighbor. As John writes with startling clarity: "Whoever does not love his brother whom he has seen cannot love God whom he has not seen" (1 John 4:20).

The command to love neighbor originates in the Torah (Leviticus 19:18), where it appears in a chapter filled with concrete social obligations: fair wages, honest dealings, protection for the vulnerable, care for the poor and the stranger. Love is not sentiment. It is enacted justice and mercy.

Jesus deepens this command in the parable of the Good Samaritan (Luke 10:25–37). The question "Who is my neighbor?" is turned on its head. Neighbor is not defined by proximity, ethnicity, or convenience. Neighbor is the one whose suffering interrupts us. To love one's neighbor is to cross boundaries and incur cost. This love is not abstract benevolence. It is embodied compassion.

The Biblical Ground
Embracing Creation

In the previous chapter, we considered reconciliation as the heart of the gospel—God restoring what sin has fractured and forming a people who embody justice and compassion. Yet reconciliation, if genuine, does not remain enclosed within the boundaries of the church. A reconciled people become a sent people.

If spiritual formation shapes us into the likeness of Christ, then that likeness must take visible form in the world Christ loves. The One who reconciles sinners is the same One through whom all things were made (John 1:3) and in whom all things hold together (Colossians 1:17). The scope of redemption is as wide as creation itself.

Thus, reconciliation necessarily unfolds into embodied witness—loving neighbor and embracing creation as acts of faithful discipleship. Scripture begins not with the salvation of souls but with the goodness of creation. "God saw everything that he had made, and behold, it was very good" (Genesis 1:31).

Humanity is placed within creation not as an exploiter but as a steward. The mandate to "have dominion" (Genesis 1:28) is often misunderstood. In the biblical imagination, dominion reflects God's own reign—life-giving, ordering, sustaining. In Genesis 2:15, humanity is placed in the garden "to work it and keep it." The Hebrew verbs imply both cultivation and protection.

Creation care, then, is not environmental trendiness; it is original vocation. The Psalms celebrate a creation that praises its Maker (Psalm 19; 104). The land is given Sabbath rest (Leviticus 25). The prophets envision not merely redeemed people but renewed earth (Isaiah 65).

The New Testament intensifies this hope. Paul writes that creation itself "has been groaning" and awaits liberation (Romans 8:19–23). Christ's reconciling work extends to "all things, whether on earth or in heaven" (Colossians 1:20). Redemption is cosmic in scope. To follow Christ, therefore, is to care about what He intends to restore.

The Incarnational Shape of Witness

The doctrine of the Incarnation anchors embodied witness. "The Word became flesh and dwelt among us" (John 1:14). God does not save from a distance. He enters creation. He eats, touches, heals, weeps. Jesus' ministry affirms the material world even as it redeems it. He multiplies bread, calms storms, and restores bodies. Salvation is not an escape from the physical but its renewal.

If spiritual formation is conformity to Christ, then it will take on an incarnational shape. It will move toward bodies, neighborhoods, systems, and ecosystems. It will resist dualism that privileges "spiritual" matters over material ones. The Christian life is lived in public.

The Early Church
Love Made Visible

The earliest Christians understood love of neighbor as integral to discipleship. In Acts 2 and 4, believers shared possessions so that "there was not a needy person among them." Economic generosity was a spiritual formation. Caring for widows (Acts 6) was not delegated away from spiritual life; it was addressed as an urgent expression of it.

During the plagues of the second and third centuries, pagan elites often fled infected cities. Christians remained to care for the sick. Dionysius of Alexandria described believers who ministered to the dying "heedless of danger." Many died in the process.

Their love was embodied witness. Christians also became known for rescuing infants abandoned in Roman society. They treated unwanted lives as image-bearing lives. Neighbor-love disrupted cultural norms.

While the early church did not use modern ecological language, its theology affirmed creation's goodness. Early theologians such as Irenaeus emphasized the material goodness of creation against Gnostic movements that despised the physical world. The doctrine of resurrection itself—bodily, not merely spiritual—affirmed the value of creation. Love of neighbor and affirmation of creation were inseparable from Christian identity.

Francis of Assisi
Joyful Poverty and Creation's Praise

Few figures embody love of neighbor and creation more vividly than Francis of Assisi. Renouncing wealth, Francis embraced voluntary poverty so that he might be free to love without possession. He cared for lepers—those society feared and rejected. In kissing a leper's diseased hand, Francis encountered Christ.

But Francis's love extended beyond human neighbors. His "Canticle of the Creatures" praises Brother Sun and Sister Moon, celebrating creation as a gift and kin. For Francis, creation was not an object to exploit but a choir joining in praise of the Creator. His life illustrates a profound truth:

spiritual formation reshapes desire. When freed from greed and fear, the heart learns to delight in both neighbor and earth.

Loving Neighbor and Creation Today

The church today continues this embodied witness in diverse ways. Congregations establish food pantries and community gardens in neighborhoods marked by scarcity. Christian physicians serve in under-resourced regions. Believers foster children and advocate for the unborn and the elderly. Churches adopt sustainable practices—reducing waste, stewarding land responsibly, recognizing that environmental degradation often harms the poor most deeply.

These actions are not distractions from prayer; they are extensions of it. When rooted in Scripture and sustained by worship, love of neighbor and care for creation become means of grace. They train attentiveness, humility, patience, and courage.

They expose idols of comfort and consumption. They confront indifference. They enlarge compassion. They shape us into a people who resemble Christ.

Embodied Witness as Spiritual Formation

To love neighbor and embrace creation is to live between the cross and the coming kingdom. Revelation ends not with escape from earth but with a renewed heaven and earth where God dwells among His people (Revelation 21–22). The tree of life reappears. The river flows. The nations are healed.

Spiritual formation prepares us for that future by training us to anticipate it now. Each act of neighbor-love becomes a sign of reconciliation. Each gesture of stewardship becomes a foretaste of restoration. Each practice of simplicity resists a culture of excess.

Embodied witness is not about saving the world by our strength. It is about living faithfully in the world God is saving.

Reconciliation births justice. Justice flows into love. Love extends to creation. And through it all, the Spirit forms us—slowly, steadily—into people whose lives testify that Christ is Lord not only of souls, but of all creation.

Reflection Questions

How does the Incarnation challenge a purely private understanding of spiritual formation?

In what ways does my love of God concretely shape my love of neighbor?

What practices of simplicity or stewardship might deepen my freedom to love?

Where do I see creation groaning in my local context—and how might I respond?

How can my church embody reconciliation not only socially, but ecologically?

What historic example (Francis, Basil, early Christians during plagues) most challenges my own discipleship?

Suggested Reading

Richard Bauckham, *Bible and Ecology* (Darton, Longman & Todd, 2009).

Wendell Berry, *The Art of the Commonplace* (Counterpoint, 2003).

Lisa Sharon Harper, *The Very Good Gospel* (WaterBrook, 2016).

Rowan Williams, *The Wound of Knowledge* (Darton, Longman & Todd, 2014).

Norman Wirzba, *Way of Love* (Baker, 2015).

Section III
Relationship with Self

Chapter 8
Knowing Yourself
Identity, Wholeness, and the Inner Journey

There was a season in my life when I wore spiritual activity like armor. I prayed often, read Scripture daily, served on church teams, volunteered where I could, yet, inside I felt hollow. Underneath the outward rhythms of faith, there was a quiet desperation, a gnawing anxiety, a fear of being unseen. I was busy for God, but deeply disconnected from myself.

One night, after yet another long day of ministry, I sat alone in a room with a journal and a candle. I didn't come with lofty expectations. I simply began to write: "Who am I, really? What am I carrying beneath the tasks and smiles and Sunday morning greetings?" The question landed harder than I expected. It felt heavy. It felt necessary. It felt true.

In that moment, I began to understand what so many saints and mystics before me had known: you cannot be spiritually mature while remaining emotionally unaware or spiritually fragmented. You can perform holiness, but you cannot live holiness without honesty.

The Journey Toward the True Self

One of the most powerful voices in modern Christian spirituality, Thomas Merton, described the inner journey as a movement from the false self, the self shaped by ego, fear, image, and performance, to the true self, the self hidden with Christ in God. "Every one of us," he wrote, "is shadowed by an illusory person: a false self. This is the man [or person] I want myself to be but who cannot exist, because God does not know anything about this person."

That illusion, the self we try to manage and present, keeps us exhausted. We build it out of reputation, success, theological correctness, or ministry output. But underneath, we may still carry fear, shame, or deep loneliness.

God is not interested in the self we pretend to be. God longs to form our real self, the one that shows up in silence, in suffering, in joy, in tears, in prayer. Merton believed that discovering the true self was not only essential to holiness, but to vocation, to peace, to love. The closer we move toward our authentic identity in God, the more truly we can love others.

Belovedness at the Center

Henri Nouwen, another guide for many weary souls, said that at the core of our formation must be one spiritual truth: You are the beloved of God. Not because of what you accomplish, not because of your ministry, not because of your purity or success, but because God has called you beloved from the beginning.

In *Life of the Beloved,* Nouwen reflects that every temptation Jesus faced in the wilderness was about identity: "If you are the Son of God…" Prove it. Show it. Earn it. But Jesus resisted. He didn't perform to be affirmed. He rested in what the Father had already spoken: "You are my Son, whom I love."

Many of us spend decades trying to earn what God has already given: love, dignity, identity. Nouwen reminds us that we must return, again and again, to that inner voice of grace: You are beloved. And from that truth, and only from that truth, can true formation begin.

Spiritual Practice
Solitude and the Inner Life

Both Merton and Nouwen agreed that one of the essential practices for knowing the self is solitude, not isolation, but the brave, silent space where we face ourselves in the presence of God.

Merton, who lived for many years in a Trappist monastery, said that solitude is not a place to escape people but to become more fully present to God, to others, and to the world. In silence, we stop curating an image. We learn to listen. We come home to what is real.

Nouwen also saw solitude as foundational for spiritual life. In solitude, he wrote, "I become aware that my worth is not dependent on what I do or how I perform." In that quiet, we are stripped of roles and masks, and slowly, lovingly, reintroduced to ourselves as God sees us.

I remember trying solitude for the first time, not in a monastery, but in a park. No phone. No book. Just stillness. At first, it felt awkward. Then it felt uncomfortable. Then it felt like home. I met God there, and in a strange way, I met myself too.

Wholeness, Healing, and the Gift of Awareness

Most of us carry wounds, old memories, silent fears, generational patterns, or buried shame. These do not disqualify us from holiness. In fact, they often become the place where grace enters most deeply.

Henri Nouwen famously called us "wounded healers," people who are not healed before they minister, but who are healed as they minister, through their wounds, with the compassion they have received.

In my life, healing came not through hiding pain, but naming it in prayer, in therapy, in silence, in friendship. Wholeness was not the absence of struggle. It was the presence of grace in the struggle.

And that is the call of the inner journey: not to escape your story, but to embrace it with Christ at the center. Not to erase your past, but to re-narrate it in light of God's love. Not to become perfect, but to become whole, fully yourself, fully alive, fully rooted in grace.

Becoming Our Truest Selves in Christ

When we begin to live from our true self and grounded in God's love, shaped by grace, no longer dominated by fear or comparison, something powerful happens. We become less defensive, more compassionate. Less anxious, more free. Less reactive, more rooted.

Our ministries stop being fueled by performance. Our relationships stop being ruled by insecurity. Our spirituality stops being a ladder and starts becoming a home.

Merton described this movement as "the recovery of one's inner truth." Nouwen called it "living from the heart of our belovedness." Jesus called it "life to the full" (John 10:10).

It is not quick. It is not easy. But it is holy. And it is possible.

Reflection Questions

Where do you see signs of the false self operating in your life, roles, fears, masks, or performances?

What has shaped your identity more: the voice of God's love or the voices of expectation, shame, and comparison?

What might it look like to begin a practice of solitude or silence, not for achievement, but for listening and resting in God's presence?

What wounds or parts of your past are you being invited to bring into the light of grace, with honesty and hope?

How would living from your true identity, the beloved of God, change how you lead, relate, serve, rest, and pray?

Suggested Reading

Augustine, *Confessions* (various editions).
Ruth Haley Barton, *Strengthening the Soul of Your Leadership* (IVP, 2012).

Thomas Merton, *New Seeds of Contemplation* (New Directions, 1972).
Thomas Merton, *No Man Is an Island* (Harcourt, Brace, 1955).
Henri Nouwen, *The Return of the Prodigal Son* (2nd ed.; Image Books, 1997).
Henri Nouwen, *Life of the Beloved* (Crossroad, 1992).
Dallas Willard, *The Spirit of the Disciplines* (HarperSanFrancisco, 1990).

Chapter 9
Sacred Rhythms
Spiritual Practices for Inner Formation

There was a time in my life when my understanding of spiritual growth centered on intensity, how much I prayed, how long I studied, how faithfully I served. I measured my faith in spiritual output. But with time and failure, I began to see that transformation doesn't come from doing more for God. It comes from being with God. Not harder work. Deeper presence.

What I lacked wasn't willpower; it was rhythm. My soul was overcommitted but undernourished. I had habits of faith, but I didn't have space for grace. I wasn't being shaped; I was just surviving.

Then I encountered the spiritual practices and ancient rhythms of rest, silence, prayer, and attention passed down through centuries of Christian tradition. These weren't rules or rituals for the rigid. They were invitations: to slow down, to listen, to make space for grace, and to allow the Holy Spirit to shape my soul.

Practices, Not Performances

The phrase "spiritual disciplines" has long been used in Christian history, but today, many find "spiritual practices" a better fit. A practice is something we return to regularly, not to prove ourselves, but to be formed. A practice makes space. It invites rhythm. It honors process.

Spiritual practices aren't about spiritual perfection. They are about presence. They help us notice God, receive love, sit in silence, tell the truth, release control, and become whole.

Church history is rich with examples. The Desert Fathers and Mothers of the 3rd and 4th centuries retreated to the wilderness to cultivate silence, simplicity, and solitude. Their goal was not to find escape, but to find clarity to hear the voice of God beneath the clutter of empire, busyness, and ego.

In the Middle Ages, Benedict of Nursia developed a *Rule of Life*, a daily rhythm of prayer, work, rest, hospitality, and silence. Benedict believed the soul was not formed by emotion but by habit. The Benedictines lived according to *ora et labora* (pray and work) a model of balance and faithfulness.

Later, figures like Ignatius of Loyola, the founder of the Jesuits, developed the *Spiritual Exercises*, which include practices of daily *examen*, imaginative prayer with Scripture, and discernment. Ignatius taught that spiritual practices are not one-size-fits-all; each person is invited to discover how they best hear and respond to God.

Julian of Norwich, Teresa of Ávila, and John of the Cross expanded these rhythms into mystical reflection, teaching that inner stillness and loving awareness of God could lead to deep union and healing.

Even reformers like Martin Luther, often associated with doctrine, practiced regular prayer, meditation, and worship as means of spiritual resilience. Luther once wrote, "I have so much to do that I shall spend the first three hours in prayer."

These voices remind us: spiritual practices are not new ideas. They are ancient gifts.

Silence and Solitude
Sacred Space for Presence

Silence was the first practice I reclaimed. Not silence for productivity, but silence for presence. Henri Nouwen called silence the "home of the word," the sacred space where God's voice becomes audible, not in thunder, but in whispers. Thomas Merton believed silence revealed the truth of who we are before God. He wrote, "In silence, God ceases to be an object and becomes an experience."

At first, silence felt like absence. But in time, I discovered it was the opposite. In silence, I wasn't performing. I wasn't managing. I was just present and God was there. Solitude followed. Not isolation, but intentional withdrawal from noise and demands. In solitude, I faced my real self, not just the "me" I wanted others to see. It was uncomfortable. But it was holy.

Sabbath
Trusting the Rhythm of Grace

Sabbath is one of the oldest spiritual practices woven into creation itself. God rested, not because God was tired, but because rest was part of being whole.

To practice Sabbath is to trust that I am not defined by productivity. It is to say "no" to urgency and yes to peace. It is to lay down the lie that I am holding the world together. Rabbi Abraham Joshua Heschel called Sabbath "a sanctuary in time." In my own life, it became that: a protected space where I could breathe deeply, eat slowly, walk gently, pray freely.

On Sabbath, I do nothing for productivity. I engage only what brings delight or stillness: reading poetry, cooking, praying slowly, being with people I love. And in those hours, I remember who I am: not a machine, not a role, not a title, but a child of God.

Prayer
More Listening Than Speaking

Prayer was the first spiritual practice I learned as a child. But for years, I misunderstood it as mostly speaking, requests, repentance, praise, words, words, words. But prayer, I discovered, is mostly listening. Teresa of Ávila said, "Prayer is nothing else than being on terms of friendship with God." Prayer is relationship. It's as simple and mysterious as sitting with someone who knows you better than you know yourself.

There are many forms of prayer: spoken prayers, written prayers, silent prayers, breath prayers, intercession, lament. Each one can help us open our soul to God.

But the most transformative shift for me was learning to pray with less control. Not managing the outcome, but sitting in presence. Not striving, but resting. Not striving to impress, but resting in love.

One of the prayers I've returned to often is from Psalm 131: "I do not occupy myself with things too great and too marvelous for me; but I have calmed and quieted my soul, like a weaned child with its mother."

That image has become prayer for me, not always eloquent, but honest. Not always confident, but trusting. Not always wordy, but always welcome.

Meditation and *Lectio Divina*
Letting Scripture Read Us

Reading the Bible is essential to Christian life. But it's easy to treat it as information instead of formation. Meditative reading (or *Lectio Divina*) helps us slow down and listen. I remember reading the words of Jesus in John 15: "Abide in me as I abide in you." I let that phrase repeat, like breath. And over time, I began to believe it. Not just in my head, but also in my spirit.

This is the goal of meditation, not to study Scripture only, but to let it study us. To let it shape our wounds and longings. To let it anchor us in grace.

Simplicity, Stillness, and the Gift of Being

Other rhythms emerged too: simplicity, which taught me to live with less and be content;

stillness, which taught me to wait; and attentiveness, which trained me to notice small graces in everyday life.

Each practice, whether it lasted five minutes or a full Sabbath day, became a way to stop striving and start receiving. Each one said, "You are already loved. You don't need to earn grace. You need to make space for it."

Spiritual formation isn't about adding more. It's about creating space for God to do what only God can do. These sacred rhythms of prayer, silence, meditation, Sabbath, and others are not ends in themselves. They are means of grace. They reorient the soul. They quiet the noise. They make room for joy.

The Long Slow Work of Spiritual Practice

Spiritual practices are not techniques to manipulate God. They are ways of opening ourselves to the reality that God is already present. They create space in our crowded hearts. They teach us to return to grace, again and again.

You don't need to master every practice. Begin with one. Silence. Prayer. Sabbath. Scripture. Simplicity. Let it sink in slowly. Don't evaluate the results. Just return. That's the rhythm. As Thomas Merton said, "We do not first see, then act. We act to discover what we see." Practice teaches us. We learn who God is and who we are as we live it out.

And as Henri Nouwen reminds us, all practices are rooted in one truth: we are the beloved of God. Every rhythm, every silence, every prayer, every breath becomes a response to that love.

Spiritual Practice Guide

Silence

Sit quietly for 5–10 minutes daily. Breathe slowly. When thoughts come, gently return to stillness. Begin with the simple inner phrase: "Be still and know."

Solitude

Set aside extended time, a half-day, a day, or weekend, for silent withdrawal (no social media, no agendas). Journal, walk, pray, or sit. Allow space for thoughts, memories, longings, grief, gratitude.

Sabbath

Choose a 24-hour (or half-day) rhythm weekly. Turn off productivity-driven activity. Rest, delight, pray, eat slowly, enjoy creation or community, reflect.

Prayer

Use breath prayers, spontaneous prayers, and Scripture-based prayers. Alternate between speaking and silence. Practice not to "get results" but to cultivate relationship.

Meditation / Lectio Divina

Select a short Scripture passage. Read slowly. Reflect on a word or phrase. Pray what arises. Rest in God's presence. Return to daily life carrying that Word.

Simplicity & Stillness

Simplify schedule, commitments, consumption. Limit distractions. Create margins. Notice rhythm of body, rest, work, and leisure, trusting that freedom and presence come before productivity.

Reflection Questions

Which practice (silence, Sabbath, prayer, meditation, simplicity) resonates most with you and why?

Which feels hardest or most foreign and what resistance or fear arises when you consider it?

What rhythms or practices could you realistically begin this week? What might make that possible (time, space, mindset)?

As you engage in a practice, what are you learning about yourself and your rhythms, needs, longings, patterns, or wounds?

Over time, how might spiritual rhythms reshape your identity from performance-driven to presence-rooted?

Suggested Reading

Anonymous, *The Cloud of Unknowing* (various editions)

Benedict of Nursia, *The Rule of St. Benedict* (various editions)

Brother Lawrence, *The Practice of the Presence of God* (various editions)

Ignatius of Loyola, *The Spiritual Exercises* (various editions)

Teresa of Ávila, *Interior Castle* (various editions)
Ruth Haley Barton, *Sacred Rhythms* (IVP, 2006).
Richard Foster, *Celebration of Discipline* (HarperSanFrancisco, 1992).
Thomas Merton, *New Seeds of Contemplation* (New Directions, 1972).
Henri Nouwen, *The Way of the Heart* (Image Books, 1997).
Marjorie J. Thompson, *Soul Feast* (Westminster John Knox Press, 2014).
Dallas Willard, *The Spirit of the Disciplines* (HarperSanFrancisco, 1990).

Chapter 10
The Wounded Healer
Emotional Healing and Spiritual Integration

Not long ago, I sat across from someone in a moment of holy honesty. He said, "I've been a Christian for years, but I still feel angry all the time. I don't even know why." I nodded. "That makes sense," I said. "Have you ever brought your anger into your prayer life?" He blinked. "You're allowed to do that?"

That conversation has stayed with me because it names a truth many of us live with but rarely admit: we carry deep emotions of grief, anxiety, shame, rage and we don't know what to do with them spiritually. We assume that faith means managing them, hiding them, or outgrowing them. But what if spiritual formation isn't about escaping emotion, but integrating it? What if the path to wholeness runs straight through our wounds?

Henri Nouwen called this journey "becoming the wounded healer." He didn't mean glorifying pain or living in victimhood. He meant that we are healed and used not despite our wounds, but through them. Our stories, our struggles, our emotional terrain become the very soil where grace takes root. We don't need to hide from our brokenness. We need to bring it into the light of love.

Wholeness Begins with Honesty

One of the great gifts of Scripture is its emotional honesty. The psalms don't hide pain. They scream it: "Why have you forsaken me?" "How long, O Lord?" "My God, I cry out by day, but you do not answer." In the laments of Jeremiah, the sorrow of Job, and the tears of Jesus we find a divine permission to be human.

Jesus weeps at the tomb of Lazarus (John 11:35). He sweats blood in Gethsemane (Luke 22:44). He cries out on the cross, "My God, why have you forsaken me?" (Mark 15:34). This isn't weakness. It's incarnation. It's the embodiment of emotional truth. And if Jesus, who was fully God, fully human, allowed grief and pain to be expressed, then so must we.

Spiritual maturity isn't emotional suppression. It's emotional integration. It means bringing our whole self, not just our strengths, into communion with God.

Emotions as Messengers

In spiritual life, we often categorize emotions: joy, peace, and gratitude are holy; anger, envy, and sadness are not. But in reality, emotions are not moral judgments; they are messengers. They signal something true about our inner world. They are invitations to pay attention.

When we avoid emotions, we become fragmented. When we listen to them, we begin to understand what needs healing, where we long for love, or what boundaries have been crossed.

Jesus often asked, "What do you want me to do for you?" It's not because He didn't know; it's because naming our inner reality is part of the healing. Naming our emotion is a form of prayer. "God, I'm afraid." "God, I'm numb." "God, I'm angry." "God, I'm tired of pretending."

Emotional honesty is not complaining; it's confession. It's the beginning of transformation.

Healing in the Presence of God

One of the most profound truths I've learned is this: healing happens in the presence of love. We are not healed by willpower or theological technique. We are healed by being held in compassion, in truth, in grace. Sometimes healing comes through solitude. Sometimes through counseling. Sometimes through tears that finally fall. Often it comes slowly like dawn after a long night.

Thomas Merton once said that the spiritual life is not about self-improvement, but about discovering the truth and allowing that truth to be transformed by God. The more we allow our inner selves to be known, the more grace can take root.

For me, healing began when I stopped hiding my shame in prayer. I stopped filtering my words. I simply said, "Here it is, God. All of it." And I heard no judgment, only love. Not permission to stay wounded, but presence in the wound. That's what made healing possible.

Integration
Becoming Whole

To be whole is not to be unbroken. It is to be integrated, to live from a center of truth and love, where nothing is hidden and nothing is wasted. This is the heart of spiritual formation. When we begin to integrate head and heart, past and present, weakness and strength, we become more compassionate. We stop projecting our wounds onto others. We stop striving to prove ourselves. We live from belovedness, not performance.

This kind of formation is slow. It requires spiritual practices, not only silence, Sabbath, and Scripture, but also confession, lament, embodiment, and healing prayer. It may involve spiritual direction or therapy, journaling or weeping. But all of it leads to love. Theologian James Finley says, "God is not someone you need to be afraid of. God is the one who was with you in the trauma holding you when you didn't know you were being held." That's the healing we need, not just for our faith, but for our humanity.

The Sacredness of the Body

Too often in Christian spirituality, we've inherited a subtle dualism, a belief that the soul is what really matters, while the body is just a temporary shell. But Scripture tells a different story. From the very beginning, we were created as embodied beings. God formed Adam from the dust and breathed life into him (Genesis 2:7). Our bodies are not incidental. They are essential.

Jesus didn't redeem souls only; He healed bodies. He touched the untouchable. He fed the hungry. He carried wounds in His own flesh. In the resurrection, His body bore the marks of crucifixion. Even glorified, Jesus was embodied. Paul writes, "Your body is a temple of the Holy Spirit... You are not your own; you were bought with a price. Therefore, glorify God in your body" (1 Corinthians 6:19–20). This is not a call to aesthetic perfection or bodily shame. It is a call to reverence. To honor the sacredness of our flesh, our hunger, our limits, and our need for rest and care.

Spiritual formation is not disembodied. It involves honoring the signals of our nervous systems, resting when tired, nourishing ourselves, moving our bodies with intention, grieving through tears, laughing with others, holding space through presence. These are not detours from formation. They are how God forms us.

Becoming Wounded Healers

We are not healed so we can boast. We are healed so we can love. Our wounds when offered to God become sources of empathy. We stop needing to fix people. We start listening with grace. We stop needing to defend ourselves. We begin offering safety. This is the paradox: the most spiritually mature people I've met are not the most successful; they're the most surrendered. They've wept. They've failed. They've let go. And in doing so, they've been transformed.

Their lives carry a quiet authority, not of perfection, but of presence. They are grounded.

They are safe. They are healing to be around. That's the kind of formation I long for. And I believe it's the kind God is offering through tears, truth, tenderness, and time.

Reflection and Practice Guide

What emotion have you been avoiding bringing into your spiritual life and why?

How do you typically respond to pain? Do you hide it, intellectualize it, ignore it, or seek to control it?

What does your body tell you about your emotional or spiritual state?

When have you experienced healing in the presence of love through prayer, relationship, or rest?

What practices might help you integrate your emotional, spiritual, and physical life: therapy, movement, rest, journaling, spiritual direction, tears?

Suggested Reading

Dan Allender, *The Cry of the Soul* (NavPress, 2015).

Ruth Haley Barton, *Strengthening the Soul of Your Leadership* (IVP, 2012).

James Finley, *The Healing Path* (Orbis, 2023).

Bessel van der Kolk, *The Body Keeps the Score* (Penguin, 2015).

Hillary McBride, *The Wisdom of Your Body* (Brazos, 2024).

Thomas Merton, *New Seeds of Contemplation* (New Directions, 1972).

Henri Nouwen, *The Inner Voice of Love* (Doubleday, 1996).
Henri Nouwen, *The Wounded Healer* (2nd ed.; Image Books, 1997).
Christine Valters Paintner, *The Wisdom of the Body* (Sorin Books, 2017).
Curt Thompson, *Anatomy of the Soul* (Salt River, 2010).
Curt Thompson, *The Soul of Shame* (IVP, 2015).

Chapter 11
Listening for the Voice of God
Discernment and Inner Wisdom

A friend once asked me, "How do you know if it's God speaking or just your own thoughts?" I smiled, not because I had a simple answer, but because I've lived that question many times. Discernment, at its heart, is the spiritual art of listening, not just hearing voices, but tuning our whole selves to the quiet guidance of the Spirit. In an age of noise, discernment is resistance. It is the decision to move slowly. To listen deeply. To act wisely, not react impulsively. Discernment is more than decision-making. It is the cultivation of attentiveness to the presence, peace, and prompting of God.

There have been seasons where I begged God for signs, asked for dreams, or over-analyzed every situation. But the longer I walk with Christ, the more I learn: discernment is not a technique. It is a posture. A life of listening. A heart tuned to the subtle movements of grace.

What Is Discernment?

One of the voices that has shaped my understanding is Henri Nouwen. He described discernment not as a clever method, but as "the discipline of listening to that small voice and trusting that God is always active and speaking, even in the most unexpected places." Discernment, for Nouwen, is a way of life, a spiritual attentiveness to the deeper stream of God's movement within us and around us. The apostle Paul captures this when he urges us: "Do not conform any longer to the pattern of this world, but be transformed by the renewing of your mind, so that you may discern what is the will of God, what is good and acceptable and perfect" (Romans 12:2).

Discernment flows from inner transformation, not cultural conformity or external pressure. True wisdom arises when the Spirit reshapes our mind, heart, and affections. But discernment is not always about answers. Sometimes, it's about presence and learning to wait, to sense, to receive, to rest in God's unfolding will. As the prophet Elijah discovered: God is often not in the wind or fire, but in the gentle whisper (see 1 Kings 19:11–12).

Inner Wisdom
The Way of Merton

Another guide on this journey is Thomas Merton, the monk whose writings on contemplative living challenged me to rediscover the value of silence. For Merton, the voice of God is most clearly heard not in dramatic revelations, but in the "still point" within the soul, that place of interior freedom where ego, fear, and ambition fall away. He wrote that a truly humble person "does not cling to any image of themselves. They are open to the truth, no matter how it may appear." Discernment, for Merton, wasn't about mastering divine secrets, but about becoming transparent to God.

Discernment of Body and Spirit

Discernment is not just cognitive. It is embodied. Our bodies carry intuition, memoria, emotion, and spiritual awareness. The Spirit often speaks through our whole being through breath, bodily tension, rest, hunger, peace, unrest. In the tradition of Scripture, we see invitations to inner examination: "Search me, O God, and know my heart; test me and know my thoughts. See if there is any hurtful way in me and lead me in the everlasting way" (Psalm 139:23–24). "Let us examine our ways and test them and return to the Lord" (Lamentations 3:40).

These ancient stories, woven into psalms, laments, prophetic cries, remind us: spiritual life is not just thought but felt. Discernment begins when we invite God to search our hearts and our bodies, to bring what is subtle into the open.

Communal Discernment
The Quaker Witness

Discernment is often thought of as personal, an internal process. But there is a deep, biblical, communal dimension as well. The wisdom of many Christians over centuries points to the need for counsel, community, and shared hearing. In the tradition of the Society of Friends (Quakers), communal discernment is practiced by gathering in silence, prayer, and attentiveness to the Spirit. No one speaks unless moved. No majority vote, no persuasion, no hurry. Instead, the assembled community waits, prays, listens until a shared sense of clarity or peace emerges.

This echoes ancient wisdom, as in Proverbs: "Without counsel plans fail, but with many advisers they succeed" (Proverbs 15:22). By inviting companions who are trusted, Spirit-tuned, honest, we add perspective, wisdom, and love to our discernment. God often whispers clearer in the hush of communal waiting than in the clamor of our own minds.

The *Examen*
A Daily Practice of Listening

Perhaps the most practical spiritual discipline for cultivating discernment is the *Examen,* developed by Ignatius of Loyola. The *Examen* is not an exam. It is a prayerful review of the day, a posture of humble self-awareness and of inviting God's light into the ordinary.

Its roots find echoes in Scripture's call to self-examination: "Examine yourselves to see whether you are in the faith; test yourselves" (2 Corinthians 13:5).

Each evening, I sit quietly and ask:

- *Where did I sense life today: love, peace, clarity?*
- *Where did I feel disconnected: anxiety, restlessness, shame, fear?*
- *What stirred gratitude, trust, beauty?*
- *Where did I hide, close off, or resist truth?*

And then: What might God be inviting me toward tomorrow?

Over time, the *Examen* forms spiritual muscles, not of perfection, but of sensitivity. It trains us to notice God's presence in the small things, the "burning of the heart" (as in Luke 24:32) even when no profound vision comes.

Discernment as a Way of Life

Discernment is not meant for one-time decisions alone. It's an ongoing way of living, a posture of attentiveness, trust, and surrender. As the writer of Proverbs reminds us: "Trust in the Lord with all your heart, and do not rely on your own insight. In all your ways acknowledge him, and he will make straight your paths" (Proverbs 3:5–6). That's what discernment teaches: not reliance on our own understanding, but trust in God who guides, reshapes, heals.

I no longer believe God's will is a tightrope to walk. It's a field of grace wide enough to walk freely, spacious enough to make mistakes, gentle enough to lead us forward step by step. Discernment is learning to walk in that field humbly, attentively, and steadily.

Reflection Questions

Where in your life are you seeking clarity or direction right now?

Which of the spiritual movements (consolation in the form of peace, hope, clarity or desolation in the form of confusion, fear, unrest) have you noticed in your recent experiences?

How might you practice trust, rather than control, in your next decision?

What does your body reveal when you sit with different options or invitations, tension, rest, anxiety, or peace?

Who in your life serves as a wise, Spirit-led companion for communal discernment?

Spiritual Practices for Discernment

Daily Examen

A brief prayerful review each evening: what gave life/how did I respond/where did I resist/what is God inviting tomorrow?

Body Listening

Sit quietly with a decision or question. Notice bodily sensations, breath, posture. Ask: does this option lead toward peace or tension?

Communal Discernment (Quaker-style)

Meet with trusted spiritual friends. Sit in silence. Invite contributions only as led by the Spirit. Listen for shared sense of clarity or peace.

Scripture Immersion

Meditate on key passages: Romans 12:2; Proverbs 3:5–6; 1 Kings 19:11–12; Psalm 139:23–24; 2 Corinthians 13:5; Luke 24:32. Ask: What is God saying in this moment? How do I respond?

Suggested Reading

Ignatius of Loyola, *The Spiritual Exercises* (various editions)

Ruth Haley Barton, *Pursuing God's Will Together* (IVP, 2012).

Adele Calhoun, *Spiritual Disciplines Handbook* (rev. ed.; IVP, 2015).
Brian Drayton, *On Living with a Concern for Gospel Ministry* (2nd ed.; Quaker Press of Friends General Conference, 2019).
Thomas Merton, *Contemplative Prayer* (Image Books, 1971).
Thomas Merton, *New Seeds of Contemplation* (New Directions, 1972).
Henri Nouwen, *Discernment: Reading the Signs of Daily Life* (SPCK, 2013).
Parker Palmer, *Let Your Life Speak* (Jossey-Bass, 2000).
Barbara Brown Taylor, *When God is Silent* (Canterbury Press, 2013).

Final Invitation

Discernment is not a formula. It is a surrender. It is saying, "Here I am, Lord. Listen, just as I am." If you lean into silence, *Examen*, communal prayer, listening to your innermost self over time, you will begin to recognize God's voice: not always loud, but steady; not always dramatic, but faithful. May your heart learn to hear the whisper. May your soul learn to trust the slow, sure guidance of grace.

Chapter 12
The Journey of Sanctification
Holiness of Heart and Life

I once pictured holiness as a distant mountaintop, a badge only the especially spiritual wore, a standard reserved for the rare, the extraordinary. But as I've walked deeper with Christ, I've come to see holiness not as a static destination, but as a path: a lifelong journey. Not one of moral perfection as a badge, but of transformation; not separation for its own sake, but alignment of heart, soul, body, mind, and life with the living God.

Sanctification is the name Christian tradition gives to this journey of becoming more like Christ. It is not self-improvement. It is not mere moral striving. It is the gracious work of God by the Spirit shaping us slowly, patiently, lovingly from the inside out. "And all of us ... are being transformed into the same image from one degree of glory to another; for this comes from the Lord, the Spirit" (2 Corinthians 3:18).

That transformation doesn't usually happen in spectacular leaps. It unfolds beautifully (and sometimes painfully) over days, months, years: through prayer and worship, through service and surrender, through rest and repentance, through joy and grief. It shapes our hearts, desires, choices, relationships, and engagement with the world.

Holiness of Heart
The Inner Call

Before holiness shows in our actions, it begins in the heart. God's call to holiness echoes throughout Scripture: "You shall be holy, for I the LORD your God am holy" (Leviticus 11:44; echoed in 1 Peter 1:16). This is not a call to perfection, but to alignment of our inner life, affections, identity, and longings as shaped by God's holiness. Holiness means more than external conformity; it means a heart molded by God's love, mercy, truth, and beauty.

To live with holiness of heart is to walk honestly before God: to admit our fears, wounds, failures; to live in vulnerability and confession. It is to seek not only correction, but healing; not only avoidance, but restoration. When grace begins in the inner person, holiness moves from performance to transformation.

Part of that transformation is becoming more like Christ: loving what Christ loves, seeing as Christ sees, living as Christ lived. Holiness of heart becomes the soil from which compassion, integrity, and love may grow in fruitfulness.

Holiness of Life
From Grace to Action

But holiness of heart is not meant to remain private. It flows outward into how we treat others, how we engage the world, how we care for creation. Genuine holiness begins inside, but is lived out loud. For the early believers, holiness was inseparable from justice, mercy, and love. It was not tidy ritualism. It was sacrificial hospitality: feeding the hungry, welcoming the stranger, bearing burdens, reaching out to widows and orphans, showing compassion to outsiders, practicing generosity, caring for creation.

To follow Christ is not only to be saved. It is to be sent. Sent into a hurting world as vessels of hope, compassion, justice, and healing. Holiness lived becomes distributed justice in forms of generosity, integrity, solidarity, and mercy. It becomes visible. It becomes a witness.

When holiness is real, it resists exploitation, greed, prejudice, and indifference. It moves toward generosity, equity, truth, healing, servanthood. It moves toward justice in institutions and relationships. Holiness becomes more than personal purity; it becomes communal transformation.

Sanctification Through the Means of Grace

What many Christians through the centuries have discovered is that sanctification rarely happens by will alone. Instead, it is fostered through what are often called the means of grace (practices, rhythms, and structures that open us to God's transforming presence). These are not optional "extras" for the spiritually elite. They are foundational pathways, quite ordinary and accessible, through which grace flows and formation happens.

Here are some of the most central means of grace, and how they function in the process of becoming holy.

Prayer & Communion with God

Prayer is the breath of the soul. In confession, praise, petition, silence and listening, we draw near to God. In intimate communion, the Spirit heals wounds, reshapes our desires, softens hearts, and aligns our longings with God's love.

Persistent prayer invites vulnerability, dependence, surrender. Over time, it breaks down self-reliance and pride. It cultivates humility, trust, and open hands. Through prayer we learn that holiness is not about "doing Christian things," but living in relationship with the living God.

Scripture & Meditation on God's Word

When we read Scripture not as a textbook but as God's living Word, we allow it to speak into our doubts, fears, identities, choices. Meditation, *lectio divina,* memorization, and reflection open our imaginations, shape our conscience, renew our minds.

Scripture roots us in truth and orients us toward Christ. It challenges injustice, calls forth love, reveals God's character, reorients our values. When the Word dwells richly within us, sanctification becomes less about human effort and more about divine formation.

Worship, Sacraments, and Community Life

God did not intend spiritual growth to happen in isolation. The community of faith gathered for worship, sacraments (Table, baptism), and shared life is the primary arena for sanctification. In community we are known, held, corrected, encouraged, challenged, and healed. We see Christ in others. We receive grace tangibly. We carry each other's burdens. We practice love, forgiveness, service, and accountability.

In the breaking of bread, in shared prayer, in corporate worship, holiness is embodied. Grace is mediated. Communion with God becomes communion with one another. We are not sanctified alone, we are sanctified together.

Service, Mercy, Justice, and Compassion in the World

The Christian life isn't meant to be comfortable. It's meant to be costly. Holiness reshapes how we view the world, how we treat the marginalized, how we steward resources, how we engage systems. Service, compassion, justice are not optional "missions." They are essential expressions of sanctification in action.

When we serve the poor, defend the oppressed, care for creation, and advocate for justice, we live holiness outwardly. We partner with God in restoring brokenness in the world. Our inner transformation becomes social transformation.

Simplicity, Rest, Creation-Care, and Sabbath Rhythms

Holiness is not only about ethics. It is about orientation, what we value, how we live, what we consume, how we rest. Simplicity frees us from material idols. Sabbath reminds us we are human beings, not human doings. Creation-care humbles us before the One who made all things.

Through these practices, our bodily lives with their consumption, rhythm, rest, and labor align with God's design. Our sanctification becomes holistic: soul and body, inner and outer, personal and communal.

Repentance, Confession, Healing, and Ongoing Grace

Sanctification does not deny brokenness. It names brokeness. It repents from it. It seeks healing. It invites honesty. And it trusts grace. In moments of failure, relapse, and despair, sanctification remains possible. The means of grace do not promise flawless performance. They promise faithful return. They open us to forgiveness, renewal, restoration, hope.

The Reality of Growth
Progress, Not Perfection

Sanctification doesn't mean we become perfect quickly. Sometimes the journey feels stalled. Temptations return. Old patterns resurface. Disappointments come. But holiness is not about a spotless record; it's about faithful perseverance. Every beloved figure of faith in Scripture struggled: Jonah ran, Peter denied, David fell, Paul wrestled. Yet in each, God's grace remained. And in each, God offered restoration, transformation, depth.

So our journey is not toward perfection, but toward maturity, toward Christlikeness, toward becoming people whose hearts, lives, and communities reflect God's love and justice. Sanctification is not about human effort alone. It's about daily cooperation with grace. It's about saying yes to God's shaping hand, over and over. It's about letting God form us, not by our own striving, but by His Spirit, through means of grace, over a lifetime.

Reflection & Practice Guide

How do you currently define holiness as moral perfection, spiritual performance, separation, or transformation by grace? What might change in your life if holiness meant becoming more like Christ in heart and life?

Where in your context do you sense God inviting you to move from inner renewal toward outward justice in the forms of compassion, generosity, service, care for creation, and solidarity with the marginalized?

Which "means of grace" (prayer, Scripture, worship, community, service, simplicity, stewardship, rest) have you neglected and which feel most alive to you now? What first step could you take to re-engage that practice?

Reflect on your journey: can you see seasons of growth, struggle, and transformation as well as times when grace shaped your heart or life, even through failure or hardship?

How might your personal holiness contribute to collective justice and healing in your family, church, community, social systems, and creation, not as duty, but as visible participation in God's redemptive work?

Suggested Reading

John Wesley, *A Plain Account of Christian Perfection* (various editions)

Timothy Keller, *Generous Justice* (Penguin, 2010).

Henri Nouwen, *Life of the Beloved* (Orbis, 1998).

R. C. Sproul, *The Holiness of God* (Tyndale House, 1985).

Section IV
Relationship with Creation

Chapter 13
Creation as Sacred
Spiritual Formation as Redemption for All Creation

The rustle of wind through the trees. The rhythm of ocean waves. The rising of the sun and the whisper of evening. All of creation sings the song of its Maker, sometimes in majesty, sometimes in groaning. From Genesis to Revelation, Scripture tells a story not only of human redemption but of cosmic restoration. God's covenant reaches beyond the human heart into the soil, sky, sea, and every living thing.

Yet for too long, Christian spirituality has been reduced to the private, the interior, the abstract. Creation with its ecosystems, creatures, resources, and rhythms has been treated as background scenery, not as sacred. This division between "spiritual" and "physical" has not only distorted our theology; it has harmed the planet. Forests are cut, waters polluted, species lost, and the poor disproportionately suffer. And the church, called to be stewards of God's good earth, too often remains silent.

But Christian spiritual formation must be creation-aware. To be formed in the image of Christ is to be formed as co-healers of a broken world. Spiritual maturity isn't just measured in personal piety, but in how we love, tend, protect, and live within creation. Redemption, at its core, is not escape from the world. It is the healing of all that God has made.

In the beginning, "God saw all that God had made, and it was very good." (Genesis 1:31). The earth was not an accident or afterthought. It was and is a work of art, imbued with divine glory. The Psalmist declares, "The heavens are telling the glory of God; and the firmament proclaims God's handiwork." Creation is not just useful; it is sacred. When God created humankind, we were placed in a garden, not a temple, not a city, not a courtroom. We were given a vocation: to till and keep. (Genesis 2:15) This Hebrew phrase implies care, stewardship, cultivation, and protection. It is a priestly task. To be human is to be a caretaker of the sacred.

Yet sin fractured that relationship, not only with God and neighbor, but with the earth itself. Where there was once harmony, there is now exploitation. But God's redemptive story does not stop with humans. Paul tells us that "creation itself will be set free from its bondage to decay… and has been groaning in labor pains until now" (Romans 8:21–22). Salvation includes the whole cosmos.

If the earth is part of God's redemptive plan, then spiritual formation must reflect that. Our practices of prayer, simplicity, hospitality, and justice must extend to creation. Every step we take toward Christ-likeness should leave a mark, not only in our inner life, but on how we live on the land, consume resources, and treat non-human life.

Contemplation that does not lead to care for creation is incomplete. Simplicity that does not confront consumerism is shallow. Worship that ignores the cries of a wounded earth is tone-deaf. When we begin to see creation as beloved and as groaning, waiting, and worthy, we engage in a new kind of discipleship: eco-discipleship. This means living with reverence for place; consuming mindfully and justly; advocating for environmental justice; integrating care for the earth into worship and teaching; and practicing spiritual disciplines that include nature and stewardship.

For centuries, Western Christianity has too often aligned with dominion and control by misreading Genesis 1:28 ("have dominion over") as permission to exploit, rather than responsibility to protect. But true dominion mirrors God's character not as domination, but as care. The Church must reclaim its prophetic voice in the ecological crisis: not as environmental activists first, but as people of faith who believe that God's love extends to all creation, and that our spiritual lives are diminished when we sever our ties to the natural world.

Spiritual formation that remains detached from creation will be stunted. But when it reconnects to the soil, the river, and the sky, it becomes full, vibrant, alive. Jesus walked among trees, taught from boats, fasted in wilderness, prayed in gardens, and stilled storms. He was born into the world, not apart from it. His resurrection body still bore the marks of the earth.

Colossians tells us that "through him God was pleased to reconcile to himself all things, whether on earth or in heaven" (Colossians 1:20). Not just souls. Not just sinners. All things. To follow Jesus, then, is to enter this ministry of reconciliation, not only with our enemies, but with the entire created order.

Reflection Questions

How have you viewed the relationship between your spiritual life and creation?

In what ways might your daily habits affirm or deny the sacredness of the earth?

Where is God inviting you into more faithful stewardship of creation?

Spiritual Practices

Nature Walk with Prayer

Spend time outdoors simply observing and thanking God for creation.

Waste Audit

Track your waste and prayerfully consider changes toward simplicity and justice.

Eco-Examen

Reflect on how your life impacts the earth and seek God's guidance for change.

Suggested Reading

Wendell Berry, *The Art of the Commonplace* (Counterpoint, 2003).

Norman Wirzba, *Food and Faith* (Cambridge University Press, 2011).
Pope Francis, *Laudato Si'* (Sunday Visitor, 2015).

Chapter 14
Simplicity, Sustainability, and the Spiritual Practice of Enough

A friend once confessed, "The more I own, the more I feel owned." It was said half-jokingly, but with a sincerity that I could feel. That single sentence reveals a deep truth about modern life: we are drowning in excess while starving for meaning. The endless pursuit of more (more comfort, more consumption, more image, more security) has not led us into abundance. It has left us exhausted, distracted, and spiritually malnourished.

Simplicity is not austerity. It's clarity. It is living with less so that we might live with more (more presence, more gratitude, more freedom, more love). Simplicity is not deprivation. It is liberation. And in Christian tradition, simplicity is not a lifestyle trend or minimalist aesthetic; it is a spiritual practice. A pathway to holiness. A sign of the kingdom. In a culture formed by overconsumption, Christian formation must offer a counter-narrative: that we were not created to hoard, compete, or possess. We were created for communion with God, with others, and with creation. Simplicity is how we begin to live into that truth.

Everywhere we turn, we are offered more: more options, more upgrades, more advertising. Our identities become entangled with what we buy. Even our spiritual lives can be shaped by the metrics of materialism, bigger ministries, newer programs, and brand-name discipleship.

Jesus never invited people into bigger, better, or flashier. He invited them to follow. He invited them to leave behind. To travel lightly. To enter a kingdom where blessedness belongs not to the wealthy, but to the poor in spirit. He warned, "Be on your guard against all kinds of greed; for one's life does not consist in the abundance of possessions" (Luke 12:15). Yet the myth of "more equals better" is hard to unlearn. It numbs our ability to desire God. It seduces us into accumulation. It creates spiritual clutter.

Simplicity is how we begin to detox from that lie. Jesus' own life was marked by freedom from possessions. He had no home, no retirement plan, no wealth portfolio. His table was shared. His clothes were ordinary. His prayers were uncluttered. When someone asked him how to inherit eternal life, he responded, "Sell what you own… and come follow me" (Mark 10:21). That was not cruelty. It was compassion, a call to let go in order to receive something better.

Simplicity, then, is not about rules. It is about relationship. It is about learning to trust that what God provides is enough. It is about training the heart to desire less so that it can desire rightly. It is the quiet practice of saying: "God, you are enough. This is enough." Simplicity is not only personal; it is profoundly ecological. Every choice we make has impact. The clothes we wear, the food we eat, and the energy we use all effect creation and neighbor. To live simply is to reduce harm. To practice justice. To care for those most affected by climate disruption, overproduction, and resource exploitation.

The early Christians believed possessions were to be held in common. The desert fathers fled materialism to find God in the silence of scarcity. Francis of Assisi embraced poverty as freedom. Today, spiritual formation requires reclaiming that prophetic voice not through guilt, but through gratitude. To live simply is to live in rhythm with creation, not in opposition to it. It is to say no to excess so we can say yes to connection. It is a form of worship.

We often think of growth as addition. More knowledge. More success. More achievement. But in the way of Jesus, growth often comes through subtraction. Simplicity is not just about owning less; it is about creating space. What we subtract often determines what we are able to receive.

Fasting is a spiritual practice meant to train our desires to hunger for what truly satisfies. In the same way, simplicity can be understood as a form of material fasting. It is the intentional act of letting go not to punish the body or reject the world, but to reawaken the soul to what is essential. We call this blessed subtraction. It is the holy practice of removing clutter, excess, noise, and consumer anxiety in order to rediscover joy, peace, and presence.

Blessed subtraction says that I don't need another version of what I already have. I am not defined by my possessions. I am more available to

God and others when I am not enslaved by stuff. Subtraction clears spiritual space. It silences the voices of scarcity. It frees us from comparison and reattaches us to enoughness.

Simplicity begins in the heart ("Seek first the kingdom") but paradoxically, kingdom values often emerge not by adding more, but by subtracting the distractions that keep us from seeing what's already there (see Matthew 6:33). In a world that markets "more" as the path to happiness, blessed subtraction is a radical act of resistance. It is saying no to a life of endless appetite. And in doing so, it makes room for gratitude, contentment, and generosity.

Simplicity is not just an attitude. It is an embodied practice. It involves conscious choices about time, money, possessions, and desires. It can be practiced through decluttering our homes to make space for hospitality and stillness; living within limits as an act of trust and faith; choosing sustainability and fairness in what we buy; saying no to constant upgrades, unnecessary purchases, or compulsive habits; and finding joy in the small, the local, the shared.

Simplicity reorients our lives around what matters, not scarcity, but sufficiency; not greed, but grace; not excess, but essence.

Reflection Questions

How do consumption, comparison, or materialism shape your sense of worth?

What would it mean to embrace "enough" in your current season?

Where might God be inviting you to live more simply for the sake of your soul and for the sake of creation?

Spiritual Practices

The Practice of Letting Go

Choose one possession to give away or release.

Sabbath Simplicity

Practice one day of rest from buying, scrolling, or spending.

Gratitude Inventory

List the things you already have that bring joy and life.

Suggested Reading

Duane Elgin, *Voluntary Simplicity* (rev. ed.; Quill, 1993).

Richard Foster, *Freedom of Simplicity* (Harper & Row, 1981).

Tish Harrison Warren, *Liturgy of the Ordinary* (IVP, 2016).

Chapter 15
Sabbath and Rest for the Land
Rhythms of Renewal for Us and Earth

I remember a Sunday years ago when I decided, almost on a whim, not to check my phone for 24 hours. I silenced the emails. I canceled errands. I simply watched the sky. I walked slowly. I sat outside under an old magnolia tree. I listened to nothing, to the wind, to birds, and to my breath. By evening, I felt a strange kind of lightness: the tight knot of anxiety loosened, the pressure of tasks slackened, and I noticed something I had forgotten: I was not the owner of this time, this land, this world. I was its guest.

That day felt like Sabbath, not just a rest for me, but a small healing for creation. It awakened something deep inside: the memory that I belong to God's good world, not as exploitative dominator, but as humble caretaker.

In theology and in life, Sabbath, understood as rest, rhythm, and reverent stillness, is more than a personal prescription. It is part of God's cosmic order. It is a rhythm woven into creation at its origin, intended for humanity and the land. To reclaim Sabbath today is to reconnect to that original covenant: with God, neighbor, and earth itself.

The Sabbath begins with creation. On the seventh day God rested from work, not from weariness, but to honor completion. God looked at all that had been made and "saw that it was very good" (Genesis 1:31), then blessed the seventh day and made it holy (Genesis 2:2–3). The land, the skies and the living beings were all included in that blessing. The Sabbath was not a gift only to humankind, but to creation itself.

Later, God's law encoded rhythmic rest for the land. The command for the "sabbatical year" where the land lies fallow, debts are forgiven, and rest is granted shows a holistic vision of rest that honors ecological limits and human dignity (see Leviticus 25). In that rhythm, the wellbeing of humanity, the land, and future generations were interwoven.

Centuries later, the prophets forecast a time of cosmic restoration in which Sabbath-like peace and flourishing would return to the earth. The arrival of that restoration remains tethered to righteousness, justice, and the renewal of all creation. For us, the Sabbath is not a nostalgic relic; it is a missional commitment. It is acknowledging that when creation groans (Romans 8:22), we need more than activism: we need holy rest, restorative rhythm, and a posture of reverence.

Too often, Christian spirituality becomes privatized, centered on personal holiness, devotional habits, and inner transformation. Yet our faith has always been embodied. God becomes flesh. Incarnates. Walks among us. Empties divine power into soil and soil into flesh.

If spiritual formation forms only our souls, we risk severing faith from the world God made. But if formation includes Sabbath (rest, rhythm, care, restraint), then our bodies, our land, our neighbors, and our ecosystems become part of that formation. Sabbath slips beyond liturgy into ecology, economics, community, and justice. Sabbath teaches a theology of limits, not scarcity born of fear, but trust rooted in grace. It says: We do not control the world. We participate in it. We tend it. We love it. And that requires restraint, care, stewardship, and humility.

Practicing Sabbath can renew both inner life and outer world: soil rested, rivers given respite, bodies healed, communities re-formed. It becomes a countercultural way ancient, sacred, healing, restorative. In a world that rarely pauses, driven by urgency, production, consumption, and distraction, Sabbath can look like a radical act of resistance. But it doesn't have to be dramatic. It can begin simply:

- *A day (or half-day) when we stop production:* no errands, no shopping, limited screen time, minimal consumption.
- *A rhythm where consumption pauses so restoration begins:* we walk, we rest, we read, we reflect, we listen.
- *A season of resource rest:* choosing periodic austerity for home, for consumption, and for waste so earth and society can breathe.
- *Corporate rhythms:* church gardens, community meals, shared rest days, ecological

Sabbath where community participates in rest together.

- *Advocacy and justice:* recognizing that Sabbath for us must include Sabbath for the land and marginalized communities who suffer from exploitation by our advocating for fair labor, sustainable farming, and just economies.

In doing so, we practice a holistic faith that recognizes that the gospel is for the healing of people and planet, not only souls.

Choosing Sabbath today costs something: productivity, convenience, consumption, comfort, cultural currency. It requires rewriting rhythms, resisting messages, rethinking habits. It may mean saying no to norms, sacrifices, and expectations. That's the cost. But Sabbath brings gifts: restoration, clarity, presence, gratitude, community, ecological renewal, spiritual depth. It reminds us we are not defined by what we produce, but by who sustains us: the Creator who made land, sky, sea, and breath. Sabbath invites us to live by sufficiency, not excess; by trust, not control; by care, not consumption.

It shapes a different kind of maturity, not just spiritual, but social and ecological. It teaches us to love God, neighbor, and creation in rhythm, in humility, in grace. When we observe Sabbath in a world obsessed with efficiency, speed, and consumption, we become a living protest against exploitation. We bear witness that there is another way, a way of rest, justice, reverence, healing.

Sabbath becomes prophetic: a sign that creation belongs to God, not to commerce. That time and being matter more than doing and having. That holiness is measured not only in spiritual virtues, but in ecological faithfulness, human dignity, community health.

Our practice of Sabbath even in small acts becomes part of the larger story of redemption and restoration. It gives the groaning earth a breath. It offers the weary soul a home. It declares that in Christ, God is redeeming not only people, but creation itself.

Reflection Questions

When was the last time you paused, not just rested, but intentionally stopped, to listen to creation and rest in it? What stopped you? What stirred you?

What areas of your life (consumption, work, rhythms) feel disconnected from Sabbath rest for you, for others, and for the earth?

How might practicing Sabbath rhythms reshape your relationship to time, resources, work, and creation?

What would it look like for your faith community to adopt rhythms of rest and restoration for land, gardens, shared meals, resource sharing, and advocacy for sustainability?

Where do you sense resistance, internal or external, to Sabbath living? What would it cost, what could be gained?

Spiritual Practices

Land Sabbath

Choose one day or half-day a month to engage in gentle activity that honors creation like walking, gardening, restoring, observing, and resting.

Consumption Sabbath

Commit to a rhythm (weekly, monthly, seasonal) of minimal consumer activity like buying, waste, media, and consumption to cultivate simplicity and restraint.

Community Care Sabbath

Join or begin a local church or neighborhood project like garden, recycling, clean-up, communal meals, resource sharing to to foster ecological health and community connection.

Creation Liturgies

Integrate creation-centered worship practices: prayers for land, skyline, oceans, animals; liturgies of gratitude for seasons and creatures; seasonal observances honoring creation's rhythms.

Suggested Reading

R. Ruth Barton, *Embracing Rhythms of Work and Rest* (IVP, 2022).

Kate H. Rademacher, *Reclaiming Rest* (Broadleaf Books, 2021).
Curtis Zackery, *Soul Rest* (Kirkdale Press, 2018).

Chapter 16
Living the Kingdom in Creation
Shalom for All Things

I often think about how Jesus began His ministry. He did not start with a theological lecture or a spiritual technique. He began with a proclamation: "The kingdom of God has come near" (Mark 1:15). Sometimes we forget how startling those words truly are. Jesus was not pointing upward toward a distant heaven. He was pointing around Him, to the world He touched, walked, breathed, and healed. In His very presence, the kingdom had broken in, not in abstraction, but in embodied, earthy reality.

Over the years, many Christians have imagined the kingdom as a spiritual place we go to after death, an escape from the brokenness of the world. But Scripture gives us a far different picture. The kingdom of God is not escape; it is restoration. It is not abandonment; it is renewal. The kingdom comes not to whisk us away from creation, but to bring *shalom* to all things.

Shalom is more than peace in the sentimental sense. It is wholeness. Harmony. Flourishing. A return to the way things are meant to be. When Jesus speaks of the kingdom, He speaks of the divine intention for creation restored with humans reconciled to God and neighbor, animals cared for, land healed, systems redeemed, relationships restored, and creation freed from its groaning.

Paul captures this beautifully in Romans 8 when he declares that "the whole creation has been groaning" and waits eagerly for liberation. Creation is not just a passive backdrop to human salvation. It participates in the story. It suffers when we suffer. It hopes when we hope. And it longs for the full revelation of God's healing. The early Christians understood this well. They saw salvation not only as forgiveness for individuals, but as the restoration of the cosmos.

This vision reaches its crest in Colossians 1, where Paul announces that in Christ, God is reconciling all things, (not only souls, not only churches, not only human communities, but all things, "whether on earth or in heaven." The scope is breathtaking. The kingdom is a cosmic renewal project, a restoration of everything fractured since Eden. *Shalom* is not private; it is universal.

When we read the Gospels with this vision in mind, Jesus' ministry takes on fresh meaning. He walks among fields, teaches about seeds and sparrows, calms storms, multiplies bread, and prays in gardens. His miracles are not interruptions of the natural order; they are signs of it being set right again. He restores bodies, relationships, and communities because this is what the kingdom looks like. Healing is the language of *shalom*. Renewal is the work of new creation.

And in the resurrection, Jesus shows us what this renewal looks like in its fullness, a transformed body, recognizable yet gloriously new, walking in a garden, speaking peace, bearing wounds yet unbound by them. His resurrection is the first bloom of a healed creation. It is God's pledge that *shalom* will come to all things.

To be a follower of Jesus, then, is to live as a citizen of this kingdom, not someday, but now. Our spiritual formation must lead us into the practices of renewal and the ways of *shalom*. Christian maturity is not measured merely by personal devotion but by participation in God's healing of the world. We are invited to become co-laborers in the reconciliation of all things, people whose lives embody the peace, justice, humility, and hope of God's kingdom.

Living this way is not always dramatic. Often it begins small, with things like paying attention to the land we inhabit, honoring the creatures that share it, reducing harm, practicing justice, seeking relational reconciliation, and resisting the forces that exploit people and planet alike. It is in the humility of listening to creation rather than endlessly extracting from it. It is in the courage of confronting systems that degrade life. It is in the tenderness of caring for the most vulnerable whether human communities or fragile ecosystems.

Shalom is not a passive feeling. It is an active, restorative, generative love that reshapes the way we move in the world. When we live this kingdom life, we become signs of hope. We become reminders that the gospel is not merely about going to heaven; it is about heaven transforming earth. Our lives become sacraments of renewal. Our choices, how we treat others, how we consume, how we rest, how we vote, how we pray, how we cultivate beauty, can become liturgies of *shalom*.

This is the sacred vocation of God's people: to join the Spirit's work of renewal wherever we are, however we can. To be agents of reconciliation in relationships, communities, systems, and ecosystems. To live as if the world matters because it matters to God. To bear witness that God's kingdom is already breaking in.

We may not see the fullness of this restoration in our lifetime. Creation still groans. Injustice still wounds. Systems still inflict harm. Yet every act of reconciliation, every gesture of care, every step toward justice, every moment of gratitude, every practice of simplicity, every movement of love becomes a seed of new creation planted in the soil of the world.

And one day, those seeds will bloom. One day, what we hope for will be revealed. As Revelation promises, heaven and earth will meet, and God will dwell with creation. Tears will be wiped away, not only from human eyes but from a suffering world. Death and decay will be no more. And *shalom,* a deep, expansive, and all-encompassing *shalom,* will fill every corner of the renewed creation.

Until that day, we live the kingdom where we are. We practice resurrection. We embody *shalom*. We join God's mission of healing, not out of fear or guilt, but out of hope that the God who began this good work will indeed bring it to completion for all things.

Reflection Questions

What images come to mind when you hear the word "*shalom*"? Where do you long to experience that wholeness?

How has your understanding of the kingdom of God shaped (or limited) how you live in relation to creation?

In what small ways can your daily life become a participation in the restoration of all things?

Spiritual Practices

Kingdom Prayer Walk

Walk through your neighborhood or a natural area, praying for signs of *shalom*. Look for beauty and brokenness; offer both in prayer.

Personal Shalom Audit

Journal how your habits of spending, consuming, resting, and relating either nurture or hinder *shalom* in your life and community.

Practice of Reconciliation

Take one step this week to repair a fractured relationship, heal a hurt, or reduce harm as a tangible act of kingdom hope.

Suggested Reading

Elizabeth A. Johnson, *Ask the Beasts* (Bloomsbury, 2014).

Sallie McFague, *A New Climate for Theology* (Fortress Press, 2013).

Jonathan Wilson-Hartgrove, *The Awakening of Hope* (Zondervan, 2012).
Norman Wirzba, *This Sacred Life* (Cambridge University Press, 2021).
Randy Woodley, *Shalom and the Community of Creation* (Eerdmans, 2012).
N. T. Wright, *Surprised by Hope* (HarperOne, 2014).

Conclusion

A Lifelong Journey of Becoming

Spiritual formation is not a class we complete or a project we perfect. It is a lifelong pilgrimage, a holy unfolding. It is the slow and sacred process by which we are shaped into the likeness of Christ for the sake of the world.

Throughout this book, we have explored the four primary relationships at the heart of Christian formation: our relationship with God, with others, with ourselves, and with creation. Each of these is a thread woven into the larger tapestry of God's redemptive work. To grow spiritually is to allow God's love to penetrate and transform every dimension of our existence; nothing is outside the reach of grace.

In our relationship with God, we learn to receive love before we perform, to abide rather than strive, to listen instead of control. We discover that God is not distant or demanding, but present, relational, and radically gracious. Through prayer, Scripture, worship, and practices of presence, we begin to live not as strangers, but as beloved children.

In our relationships with others, we learn that spirituality is never solitary. Community is not a threat to holiness; it is its crucible. Forgiveness, compassion, reconciliation, and hospitality are not extra credit for the spiritual elite; they are the terrain of formation. As John Wesley reminded us, "There is no personal holiness without social holiness." We are shaped in the company of others, especially in the hard and beautiful work of loving those who are not like us.

In our relationship with ourselves, we learn to attend to the inner life with honesty and grace. We embrace our stories, confront our wounds, honor our bodies, and surrender our illusions. We no longer hide behind achievement or shame. We live as whole, integrated people who are deeply known and deeply loved by God.

And in our relationship with creation, we learn that the earth is not disposable scenery but sacred sanctuary. We are called not only to care for the planet, but to live as part of it, humbly, justly, and reverently. Spiritual formation is not complete until it reorients how we live on this earth with simplicity, with restraint, with a heart tuned to the groaning and glory of the world around us.

Each of these relationships is a doorway into transformation. And none can be neglected without deforming the others. The journey of spiritual formation, then, is a journey into wholeness, a life where love is no longer abstract, but embodied and no longer private, but public and no longer someday, but now.

This journey is not easy. It requires unlearning as much as learning. It demands vulnerability, patience, and trust. But it is also marked by joy. It is the joy of becoming more human, more present, more alive. It is the joy of participating in what God is already doing by reconciling, restoring, and renewing all things in Christ.

You do not walk this path alone. You are surrounded by a great cloud of witnesses (the saints, mystics, mothers and fathers of the faith, friends and mentors, and communities of grace). You are held by the Spirit who leads you deeper into the heart of God. And you are invited, not forced, to walk this road with courage and with curiosity.

So wherever you are in the journey, beginning, returning, weary, or awakening, may you know this: God is forming you. Slowly. Faithfully. Beautifully. Not just for your own sake., but also for the sake of the world God so loves.

May Christ be formed in you.

May love take root in you.

May you live fully, freely, and faithfully for the glory of God and the flourishing of all creation. Amen.

www.ingramcontent.com/pod-product-compliance
Lightning Source LLC
LaVergne TN
LVHW020631100826
845148LV00012B/2136

* 9 7 9 8 8 9 7 3 1 2 9 8 6 *